JUNGLE ANIMALS

A SPOTTER'S GUIDE

EARTHAWARE
KIDS

Written by: Jane Wilsher
Consultant: Barbara Taylor

Illustrated by: Lisa Alderson, Fiona Osbaldstone, Peter Bull Art Studio, Martim Camm, Alistair Barnard, Thornton Artists UK, FOLIO, Creative Communications, James McKinnon, Kevin Stead, Trevor Weeks, WA/Pricilla Barrett

Designed by: Tory Gordon-Harris

Edited by: Penelope Arlon

EARTHAWARE
K I D S

Published by EarthAware Kids

Created by Weldon Owen Children's Books
A subsidiary of Insight International, L.P.
PO Box 3088
San Rafael, CA 94912
www.insighteditions.com

Weldon Owen Children's Books:

Publisher: Sue Grabham
Art Director: Stuart Smith
Assistant Editor: Pandita Geary

Insight Editions:
Publisher: Raoul Goff
Executive Director, Kids: Kate Jerome

ISBN: 978-1-68188-766-1

Manufactured, printed and assembled in China

First printing, January 2021. TMT0121

23 22 21 20 19 1 2 3 4 5

JUNGLE ANIMALS

A SPOTTER'S GUIDE

JANE WILSHER

CONTENTS

8 **WELCOME TO THE JUNGLE**

10 In the jungle

10 **MAMMALS**

14 How to spot mammals

16 Sloths

18 Giant ground pangolin, Giant armadillo

19 Giant anteater

20 Tree shrews

22 Common vampire bat

23 Honduran white bat

24 Colugos

25 Ring-tailed lemur

26 Indri

27 Aye-aye

28 Potto, Demidoff galago

29 Western tarsier

30 Cotton-top tamarin

31 Owl monkey

32 Red howler monkey

33 Black spider monkey

34 Proboscis monkey

35 Mandrill

36 Gibbons

37 Siamang

38 Orangutan

39 Western lowland gorilla

40 Chimpanzee

42 Bonobo

43 Sun bear

44 Sloth bear

45 South American coati

46 Bengal tiger

47 Jaguar

48 Leopard

49 Clouded leopard

50 Ocelot

51 Fishing cat

52 Asian elephant

53 African forest elephant

54 West Indian manatee

55 Amazonian manatee

56 Brazilian tapir

57 Malayan tapir

58 Sumatran rhino

59 Chevrotains

60 Zebra duiker

61 Pygmy hippopotamus

62 Capybara

63 Bicolor-spined porcupine

64 Lowland paca

65 Agoutis

66 Platypus

67 Echidnas

68 Common spotted cuscus

69 Possums

70 Goodfellow's tree kangaroo

71 Bennett's tree kangaroo

72 BIRDS

74 How to spot birds

76 Cassowary

77 Great curassow

78 Indian peafowl

80 Congo serpent eagle

81 Philippine eagle

82 Hoatzin

83 Sunbittern

84 Victoria crowned pigeon

85 Nicobar pigeon,
Superb fruit dove

86 Parrots

88 Macaws

89 Kakapo

90 Pesquet's parrot

91 Red-fan parrot

92 Salmon-crested cockatoo

93 Jacamars, Rufous woodpecker

94 Trogons

95 Great blue turaco

96 Toco toucan

97 Great hornbill

98 Hummingbirds

100 Guianan cock-of-the-rock

101 Manakins

102 Broadbills

103 Superb lyrebird

104 Bowerbirds

106 Birds of paradise

108 Raggiana bird of paradise

110 REPTILES

112 How to spot reptiles

114 River turtles

116 Black caiman

117 Green iguana

118 Green basilisk lizard

119 Chinese water dragon

120 Common green forest lizard

121 Parson's chameleon

122 Kuhl's flying gecko

123 Emerald tree monitor

124 Komodo dragon

126 Green anaconda

127 Tree snakes

128 Common boa constrictor

129 Cook's tree boa

130 Milk snake

131 Mangrove snake

132 King cobra

133 Vipers

134 AMPHIBIANS

136 How to spot amphibians

138 Caecilians

139 Surinam toad

140 Tree frogs

142 Goliath frog, Coqui

143 Glass frogs

144 Poison arrow frogs

146 Wallace's flying frog

147 Hairy frog

148 FISH

150 How to spot fish

152 Splash tetra

153 Marbled hatchetfish

154 Electric eel

155 Piranhas

156 Freshwater angelfish

157 Arapaima

158 INVERTEBRATES

160 How to spot invertebrates

162 Spiders

164 Mantids

165 Spiny devil walking stick

166 Ants

168 Beetles

170 Butterflies and moths

172 Giant Atlas moth

173 Peanut-headed lanternfly

174 INDEX

WELCOME TO THE JUNGLE

Picture this—you're in the jungle and it's hot. While insects scuttle at your feet, you point your binoculars upward to an emerald tree boa dangling from a tree and a hummingbird drinking from a flower. Is that an indri climbing up high?

What will you see on your imaginary jungle adventure?

Ant

Tiger

Harlequin poison dart frog

**Emerald
tree boa**

Precious habitat

In this book you will meet
many rare and endangered
animals. Tigers, hummingbirds,
sloths, orangutans, tree frogs,
indris and lots of other creatures
are in danger because people
are cutting down their precious
rainforest home. Learn about why
these jungle animals are endangered
and the conservation projects that
are trying to save them.
Perhaps one day you
will be able to
help to protect
them too.

Indri

**Common
praying
mantis**

**Bee
hummingbird**

IN THE JUNGLE

Turn the pages of this book to discover how to track and spot all kinds of jungle animals. Imagine that you are really there, surrounded by wild vegetation. You are dripping wet from a downpour and sweating in the heat. Jungles grow near the hot Equator, which is an imaginary line around the center of the Earth. There are three kinds of jungle in this book.

Blue morpho butterfly

Monsoon rainforest
In the dry season, trees in the monsoon rainforest drop their leaves.

Lowland rainforest
The hottest, wettest rainforest grows around the Equator. It is hot and wet all year round and there are no seasons.

NORTH AMERICA

EUROPE

EQUATOR

CENTRAL AMERICA

AFRICA

SOUTH ASIA

SOUTHEAST ASIA

PACIFIC OCEAN

JUNGLE

SOUTH AMERICA

INDIAN OCEAN

ATLANTIC OCEAN

AUSTRALIA

SOUTHERN OCEAN

Mangrove forest
These forests grow on tropical coasts. Bumpy roots loop above the swampy ground.

Golden poison dart frog

Kuhl's flying gecko

ANIMAL SPOTTING

Follow these simple steps and you will be an expert jungle animal spotter in no time.

1. Start by looking up your favourite jungle animals in the index on page 174. Each animal in the book has an entry.

2. Look at the detailed artworks. Arrows and labels point to special features.

3. Look out for extra facts in the colored circles. There are WILD facts at the bottom of the pages, too.

This cockatoo's beak is so powerful it can crack a coconut.

IN DANGER
Many people are trying to protect these cockatoos by stopping them from being sold as pets.

WHERE IN THE WORLD?

LIVES: lowland rainforest, eastern Indonesia

EATS: seeds, nuts, fruit and insects

STATUS:
vulnerable

HOW BIG?

 40–50cm (16–20in) long

4. Find your bearings on the world map. See where the animals live and in what kind of jungle.

5. Many jungle animals are endangered. Look at their danger status here.

6. Compare the size of the animal with the size of a person.

Salmon crested cockatoo

IT'S WILD! Rainforests cover a small part of the Earth's surface, but more than half of the world's different types of animals live there.

MAMMALS

HOW TO SPOT MAMMALS

From a leaping lemur and a swinging monkey to a climbing cat and a swimming manatee, there are lots of mammals to spot in the jungle. These animals move in different ways and live in different places, but all share similar features. They belong to a group of animals called mammals.

Listen!
The lemur makes all kinds of noises, from shrieks and grunts to barks and howls.

What's that smell?
The lemur sprays a powerful, musky smell to mark its territory.

Use your senses
Picture this—you're standing in a jungle clearing hoping to spot a ring-tailed lemur. Look, listen and smell. You might be lucky!

Be ready
Find out when animals are up and about. The ring-tailed lemur is active during the day.

Keep your eyes peeled
Look for the ring-tailed lemur's stripy, bushy tail dangling down between the branches.

Ring-tailed lemur

WHAT MAKES A MAMMAL?

YOUNG A female mammal gives birth to live young.

MILK A baby drinks its mother's milk.

HAIR All mammals have a layer of hair or fur on their skin.

WARM-BLOODED A mammal is warm-blooded, which means it keeps its body at the same warm temperature no matter how hot or cold its surroundings.

VERTEBRATE A mammal is a vertebrate, which means it has a backbone for support.

Where do mammals live?
Mammals can be found all over the rainforest, from the very tops of the trees to the branches and ground below. They have special features to help them move, feed and hide in the forest's trees and rivers.

MAMMAL WATCH

Imagine taking a real trip into a rainforest nature reserve. A local guide knows the best place to watch safely while mammals hunt, sleep and look after their young.

On the move
The black spider monkey's tail grips the high branches so it can swing through the trees.

Blending in
A jaguar's coat blends in with the dappled shadows of the trees. This is called camouflage.

Finding food
A manatee feeds on river grasses. It grasps the blades of grass in its flippers then moves them toward its split lip to eat.

SLOTHS

As you hike across the forest floor, look up into the trees. Can you make out the shape of a shaggy-coated sloth? It is difficult to see, but the sloth is the slowest animal in the world, so once you've spotted one, it won't scamper off!

The coat hanger–shaped hands grip onto branches.

Two layers of fur keep the sloth warm and dry.

IN DANGER

The pygmy sloth is in danger of extinction. Conservation projects are trying to help save its forest home.

Moths live on the sloth's shaggy fur.

Pygmy sloth

WHERE IN THE WORLD?

LIVES: lowland rainforest and mangrove forests

◉ Pygmy sloth, Isla Escudo de Veraguas

◉ Pale-throated three-toed sloth, northern South America

◉ Maned three-toed sloth, Brazil

EATS: leaves, twigs and buds

STATUS:

◣ Pale-throated three-toed sloth – least concern

◣ Maned three-toed sloth – vulnerable

◣ Pygmy sloth – critically endangered

HOW BIG?

Pale-throated and maned three-toed sloths 55–75cm (22–30in) long

Pygmy sloth 45–53cm (18–21in) long

Maned three-toed sloth

Pale-throated three-toed sloth

A green plant, called algae, grows on the sloth's fur. It helps to camouflage the sloth in the trees.

Long, curved claws grip onto branches so tightly that the sloth can sleep upside down safely.

Head-turner

The sloth has an extra bone in its neck, which means it can turn its head almost the whole way around. But it does this slowly.

GIANT GROUND PANGOLIN

There's a chance you might see some really extraordinary creatures on your expedition. This giant ground pangolin looks like it comes from the time of the dinosaurs. Pangolins are the only mammals alive today with horny body scales.

Hard, overlapping scales keep the pangolin safe from predators. It can roll itself into a ball, too.

Giant ground pangolin

Sharp claws dig burrows, where the pangolin keeps cool during the day.

WHERE IN THE WORLD?

LIVES: lowland rainforest, West and Central Africa

EATS: insects

STATUS: vulnerable

HOW BIG?

100cm (39in) long

GIANT ARMADILLO

WHERE IN THE WORLD?

LIVES: lowland rainforest, northern South America

EATS: mainly termites, but also ants, worms and spiders

STATUS: vulnerable

HOW BIG?

75–100cm (30–39in) long

To track a giant armadillo, look for scratch marks near a termite mound, where it rakes the soil with huge front claws. The middle claw is shaped like a blade and scoops out the termites to eat.

DON'T MISS!

Look for a giant armadillo standing on its back legs. It balances on its tail to raid a tall termite nest.

Giant armadillo

Up to one hundred peg-shaped teeth mash up food.

Horny skin covers hard, bony plates.

GIANT ANTEATER

The best way to see a giant anteater is to find an ants' nest. The anteater uses its powerful sense of smell to find a nest, which it tears open with its sharp claws. In goes its snout, then its long, sticky tongue laps up thousands of ants. The anteater always leaves some ants to build the colony again so it can return for another meal.

SPOTTER FACT

An anteater eats up to 35,000 ants or termites a day. It has to eat quickly before it is stung!

WHERE IN THE WORLD?

LIVES: lowland rainforest, Central and South America

EATS: mostly termites and ants, but also worms and insect larvae

STATUS
🍃 vulnerable

HOW BIG?

100–120cm (39–47in) long

Piggyback
An anteater pup lives with its mother for two years. It hitches a ride on its mother's back.

Thick skin and long hair protect the anteater from stings and bites.

The anteater's hairy, bushy tail is often used as a blanket or sunshade.

The tongue is as long as your arm.

Giant anteater

IT'S WILD! An anteater is an excellent swimmer. It uses its snout like a snorkel.

TREE SHREWS

Ears pricked up and a nose ready to sniff out trouble, a tree shrew is always alert. Predatory snakes and birds are usually nearby. Watch quietly as the tree shrew eats, sitting on its back legs, ready to dart away. It might even make short jumps from branch to branch.

Families of tree shrews scamper along branches all day, searching out insects to eat.

Philippine tree shrew

Common tree shrew

A long tail helps the tree shrew to balance in the tall trees.

WHERE IN THE WORLD?

LIVES: lowland rainforests
- ◉ Philippine tree shrew, the Philippines
- ● Pen-tailed tree shrew, large tree shrew and common tree shrew, Malaysia and Indonesia

EATS: Insects and other invertebrates, fruit and leaves

STATUS:
🍃 least concern

HOW BIG?

10–22cm (4–9in) long

SPOTTER FACT

Before a mother goes hunting, she marks her babies with a smelly scent so that she can find them again.

The pen-tailed shrew is nocturnal, which means it comes out only at night.

Sharp claws and spread-out toes can grip firmly onto tree bark.

Pen-tailed tree shrew

The tree shrew's sensitive tail is used to "feel" around at night.

Excellent sight and smell help the tree shrew to root out insects with its snout.

Large ear holes help the shrew to hear predators nearby.

DON'T MISS!

Tree shrews can be found in lots of different places— both up in the trees and down on the jungle floor.

The pen-tailed shrew is the only tree shrew to have fine, featherlike hairs at the end of its tail.

Large tree shrew

Heat sensors on the bat's nose guide it to warm, sleeping animals.

A bat is the only mammal that can fly.

Common vampire bat

Strong back legs help the bat to climb onto large victims.

SPOTTER FACT

If the vampire bat doesn't feed for three days it will die. Well-fed bats vomit up blood to feed other hungry bats.

COMMON VAMPIRE BAT

With a thirst for blood, the vampire bat wakes as the sun sets. This bat is the only mammal that feeds on nothing but blood. Sleeping animals, such as horses, cows and pigs, are favorite targets. A vampire bat has special chemicals in its saliva that help its prey's blood flow.

WHERE IN THE WORLD?

LIVES: lowland rainforest, Central and South America

EATS: feeds on blood from mammals, such as cattle and horses

STATUS: least concern

HOW BIG?

6.5–9cm (2.5–3.5in) long

Lapping it up
Razor-sharp teeth slice a flap of flesh and the tongue laps up the blood for about thirty minutes. It doesn't even wake up its victim.

IT'S WILD! After a meal, a common vampire can be double its original weight.

HONDURAN WHITE BAT

Take care if you come across a small, folded leaf. It might be the home of a family of Honduran white bats. Rather than hanging in a cave or from a branch, they cut parts of a leaf and fold it over to make a tent.

Safe up high
During the day, as many as twelve tiny bats hide together high up in the trees. They come out at night to find fruit to eat.

The bats roost upside down in the center of the leaf.

The leaf tent keeps the bats safe from predators, as well as from the rain and hot sun.

When the sun shines through the green leaf tent, the white fur looks green. This is good for camouflage.

Honduran white bat

DON'T MISS!
Look for the Honduran white bat's curious-shaped nose. Often, this bat is called the leaf-nosed bat.

This tiny bat is about the length of your thumb.

IT'S WILD! This bat is one of only three species of bat that is completely white.

COLUGOS

Look up! If you're lucky, you might spot a colugo gliding above you from tree to tree. But don't be fooled by its nickname "flying lemur." This animal isn't a lemur and it doesn't fly. A colugo spends its life in trees, climbing and gliding at night in search of leaves and fruits.

A light skeleton with thin bones helps a colugo to stay in the air longer.

Large eyes help a colugo to see at night to make precise landings.

The gliding flaps of skin also make a hammock for a baby.

Malayan flying lemur

Animal kite
A colugo glides using huge flaps of skin that stretch from its face, across its arms and legs, to the end of its tail.

Sharp claws cling to the bark as the colugo lands.

Philippine flying lemur

DON'T MISS!
At dusk, watch a colugo glide through the trees. Spot a baby clinging to its mother's back.

WHERE IN THE WORLD?

LIVES: lowland rainforest, Southeast Asia

EATS: young leaves, shoots, fruit and leaves

STATUS:
🖎 least concern

HOW BIG?

35–42cm (14–16.5in) long

IT'S WILD! A colugo can glide over half the length of a soccer field!

RING-TAILED LEMUR

If you see one ring-tailed lemur, look nearby for the rest of the family, or troop. A female lemur is in charge of up to twenty animals. A female gives birth to one or two babies, then the whole group looks after the youngsters.

Notice the black rings around the eyes.

The upright, stripy tail makes the lemur easy for family members to spot.

Ring-tailed lemur

The tail can't grip branches. It is just used for balance and communication.

Smelly marker
The male marks his territory with a powerful smell that he makes in his scent glands.

WHERE IN THE WORLD?

LIVES: lowland rainforest and monsoon forest, Madagascar

EATS: fruit and leaves, particularly those of the tamarind tree.

STATUS:
🌿 endangered

HOW BIG?

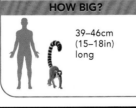

39–46cm (15–18in) long

DON'T MISS!

Watch male lemurs having a stink fight. They wipe their tails with their scent and flick it at each other!

IT'S WILD! A ring-tailed lemur's tail is longer than its body.

INDRI

You might hear this noisy lemur before you see it. During the day, the indri leaps through the trees, looking for fruit and flowers. It makes extremely loud wailing calls, telling other groups of indris to keep away.

The indri marks territory with scent glands in the cheeks.

An indri uses its hands to bring a leafy branch to its mouth, then strips off the leaves with its teeth.

The indri is the biggest lemur in the world.

Strong back legs, stout thumbs and big toes help the indri to launch and land.

Indri

WHERE IN THE WORLD?

LIVES: lowland rainforest and monsoon forest, Madagascar

EATS: young leaves, flowers, seeds, fruit and bark

STATUS:
◣ critically endangered

HOW BIG?

60–90cm
(24–35in) long

SPOTTER FACT

To warn of danger overhead, an indri roars. A honk means there's a threat on the ground.

IT'S WILD! When the indri leaps through the air, it glides upright, as if standing up.

Big eyes and ears are good for night hunting.

An aye-aye has sharp teeth that never stop growing. To keep the teeth short, it gnaws the trees.

WHERE IN THE WORLD?

LIVES: lowland rainforest and monsoon forest, Madagascar

EATS: seeds, fruit, nectar, fungi, insect larvae and honey

STATUS:
🔖 endangered

HOW BIG?

36–43cm (14–17in) long

An extremely long middle finger digs holes into tree bark to pick out grubs.

Aye-aye

Long fingers
Unusually long claws on jointed fingers are designed for gripping and cracking open bark.

An aye-aye's bushy tail has the longest fur of any lemur.

AYE-AYE

The best place to find this strange lemur is at the tops of trees among the leaves. The best time to see it is at night, when it comes out to feed. The aye-aye has an unusual way of hunting. It taps tree bark with its long middle finger and listens for echoes that let it know if there is a grub beneath.

DON'T MISS!

Listen for the aye-aye tapping a tree with its long finger to find grubs.

POTTO

The chances are, if you see a potto, it's seen you first. A potto is very slow and very quiet. When it is alarmed by a predator, it freezes, keeping completely still. If anxious, the potto tucks in its head and shows its unusual skin-covered spines on the back of its neck.

Potto

Scent glands under the potto's tail give off a smell to mark its territory.

WHERE IN THE WORLD?

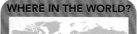

LIVES: lowland rainforest, Central Africa

EATS: insects

STATUS: least concern

HOW BIG?

30–40cm (12–16in) long

SPOTTER FACT

The potto moves so slowly and quietly that it is known as the "softly-softly" in Africa.

Look for the short finger on each hand.

DEMIDOFF GALAGO

WHERE IN THE WORLD?

LIVES: lowland rainforest, Central Africa

EATS: beetles, moths, fruit

STATUS: least concern

HOW BIG?

10–12cm (4–5in) long

SPOTTER FACT

Watch at dusk. The galago spends time yawning, grooming and stretching before it starts its hunt.

Set out at night if you want to spot a Demidoff galago, also known as a bushbaby. But keep still. The galago's ears move separately to hear the quietest sounds. Its huge eyes can spot tiny movements in dim light.

A lightweight body helps the bushbaby leap onto thin branches.

Demidoff galago

Long back legs help the bushbaby to make huge jumps.

WESTERN TARSIER

The tarsier's eyes are as big as its brain.

If you see the western tarsier, watch closely. In a split second, the tarsier will launch itself away from the branch. It can leap forty times its own body length. A tarsier's long fingers are tipped with sticky pads to grip branches. Its huge eyes will spot you in the fading light.

Western tarsier

The back legs are twice as long as its body and perfect for leaping.

A western tarsier has a smooth tail. Other tarsiers have hairy tails.

WHERE IN THE WORLD?

LIVES: lowland rainforest, islands of Southeast Asia, including the Philippines

EATS: insects, spiders, and small vertebrates, such as lizards and birds

STATUS:
✎ vulnerable

HOW BIG?

9.5–14cm (4–5.5in) long

IN DANGER!

Tarsiers are rare. They look cute, so poachers capture them to sell as pets.

IT'S WILD! A western tarsier can turn its head completely around to the back to see in all directions!

COTTON-TOP TAMARIN

If you're out early in the dawn mist, you might see cotton-top tamarins. As the sun rises, they set off to find food. The tamarins move away in small groups from the nests they have made in the branches. These monkeys swing through the trees searching for insects, fruit and white tree sap, called gum.

The tamarin raises its white mane to scare other animals away.

WHERE IN THE WORLD?

LIVES: lowland rainforest, northwestern Colombia

EATS: insects, fruit and gum

STATUS:
critically endangered

HOW BIG?

20–25cm (8–10in) long

Cotton-top tamarin

DON'T MISS!

Watch for the grooming sessions. Tamarins comb each other's coats with their long fingernails.

The tamarin's nails are shaped like claws, which are good for climbing trees.

OWL MONKEY

Head out for a late-night hike to find the noisy owl monkeys. Listen as they leap across the treetops, grunting and screeching. They are the only monkeys that hunt at night, so there is no mistaking them. Look for their big eyes and long, dangling tails.

SPOTTER FACT
During the day, owl monkeys sleep. They make beds out of leaves between branches high up in the trees.

Night eyes
Enormous eyes help the owl monkey to see at night. But it can only see in black and white.

A sharp sense of smell helps the owl monkey to sniff out food in the low light.

Colored fur camouflages the monkeys in the darkness.

A long tail helps with balance.

SPOTTER FACT
Owl monkeys are also known as "night monkeys" because they hunt at night.

Owl monkey

WHERE IN THE WORLD?

LIVES: lowland rainforest, Panama to South Amerca

EATS: mostly fruit, but also leaves and insects

STATUS:

🖊 least concern

HOW BIG?

24–37cm (9–15in) long

IT'S WILD! The male owl monkey is the main baby carrier. Soon after the baby is born, the male takes care of it almost all the time.

RED HOWLER MONKEY

At dawn, across the rainforest, a troop of red howler monkeys starts a wild, howling chit-chat. You can hear the calls from far away. The noise is deafening. They are letting other troops know where they are and warning them to keep away.

WHERE IN THE WORLD?

LIVES: lowland rainforest, northern South America

EATS: leaves, fruit, flowers, nuts, small animals and eggs

STATUS:
 least concern

HOW BIG?

60–90cm (24–35in) long

The red howler monkey is heavier and slower than other monkeys.

The howler monkey's tail acts as an extra limb, gripping the branches, like a hand.

Strong hands allow the howler monkey to swing from branch to branch.

Red howler monkey

Loud calls
Howler monkeys are some of the loudest animals on Earth. They scream to each other to try to stop fights about food and territory.

IT'S WILD! Ancient Mayan tribes worshipped howler monkeys as gods.

BLACK SPIDER MONKEY

One blink and it's gone! The black spider monkey whooshes through the trees, swinging from the branches. It grips with all its long limbs and its tail, too. The spider monkey often hangs from a branch upside down with arms, legs or its tail dangling, which makes it look like a leggy spider.

The monkey's tail has no hair on the underside for an extra-good grip on a branch.

Black spider monkey

A black spider monkey has no thumbs. Four long fingers act as hooks over the branches.

Spider monkeys are friendly to other troops. They hug to greet each other.

WHERE IN THE WORLD?

LIVES: lowland rainforest, northern South America

EATS: termites, grubs, leaves, flowers, berries and fruit

STATUS: vulnerable

HOW BIG?

40–60cm (16–24in) long

IN DANGER

Huge areas of the Amazon rainforest are being cut down every day. Spider monkeys are losing their homes.

King of the swingers
Spider monkeys can swing and race through the trees at twice the speed of a running Olympic athlete.

PROBOSCIS MONKEY

You can't mistake a proboscis monkey, because of its long, droopy nose. Wait patiently by a river or swamp and you might just see a proboscis monkey doing a belly flop. This monkey is a fast swimmer, even outswimming crocodiles.

The adult monkey has a pink nose, but it is born with a bright blue one.

Powerful arms, legs and a tail are essential for leaping and swinging.

Webbing, or stretchy skin, between the fingers helps this monkey to swim.

Proboscis monkey

WHERE IN THE WORLD?

LIVES: mangrove forest, Borneo

EATS: fruit, leaves, flowers and sometimes insects

STATUS:
🍃 endangered

HOW BIG?

53–76cm
(21–30in) long

DON'T MISS!

Listen for the honking warning call of the proboscis monkey. It is thought that its nose makes the noise extra loud.

IT'S WILD! Proboscis monkeys walking on two legs have been mistaken for humans!

MANDRILL

If you spot a brightly colored face and bottom, then the chances are you've seen a mandrill. It is the largest of the monkeys and lives in troops of about 250 animals. During the day, a mandrill roams around the ground. At night, it takes shelter in the trees.

Thick pads on the bottom support its weight when it is sitting.

A mandrill is super noisy. It grunts, screams and roars.

Powerful male
A male is larger than a female and has brighter colors on its face and bottom. He also has a yellow beard.

Toothy grin
It may not look like it, but a mandrill baring its teeth is often a friendly greeting to another mandrill.

A male has a brighter face and bottom.

Mandrill

WHERE IN THE WORLD?

LIVES: lowland rainforest, west Central Africa

EATS: fruit, leaves, liana vines, bark, stems, frogs, lizards, snakes and worms

STATUS: vulnerable

HOW BIG?

95–110cm (37–43in) long

GIBBONS

Watch daredevil gibbon acrobatics high up in the trees. Gibbons belong to a group of animals called apes. You can spot apes because, unlike monkeys, they do not have tails.

Lar gibbon

A lar gibbon has a white ring around its face.

Black crested gibbon

A male black crested gibbon is black, but a female is golden.

WHERE IN THE WORLD?

LIVES: lowland rainforest

● Lar gibbon, Laos, Malaysia, Myanmar, Thailand, Indonesia

◉ Black crested gibbon, China, Laos, Vietnam

EATS: 60% fruit, also leaves, twigs, insects and bird eggs

STATUS:

🌿 Lar gibbon – endangered

🌿 Black crested gibbon – critically endangered

HOW BIG?

Both gibbons 45–65cm (18–26in) long

Tree swinger
A gibbon uses its long arms and hooked fingers to swing gracefully through the trees. At full speed, it is as fast as a galloping racehorse.

SPOTTER FACT

A gibbon is a lesser ape. Humans, gorillas, chimpanzees, bonobos and orangutans are great apes.

SIAMANG

Listen for a male siamang singing first thing in the morning. To mark out his territory, this gibbon puffs up his throat into a ball and sings loudly for up to half an hour. He also sings "love duets" with a female.

Often, the siamang dangles by one arm and feeds.

IN DANGER

Like many gibbons, siamangs are endangered. Their homes are being destroyed for mining and farming.

The siamang has webbing between its second and third toes. No one knows why.

The vocal throat sac can inflate as large as a grapefruit.

Siamang

WHERE IN THE WORLD?

LIVES: lowland rainforest, Sumatra, Thailand and Malaysia

EATS: 160 species of plant, from vines to woody plants and figs

STATUS:
endangered

HOW BIG?

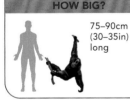

75–90cm (30–35in) long

A gibbon can walk on two legs on the ground, but it is quicker swinging through the trees using its limbs.

The siamang is the largest of all the gibbons.

A siamang can scoop up water to drink in its hands.

ORANGUTAN

Imagine your toes never touching the ground. An orangutan spends most of its life high up in the canopy. It swings by its long arms, picking fruit from the very tops of the trees. If you're lucky you may see one making a nest out of leaves in the trees.

The fur blazes orange in the sun. In the shade, it acts as camouflage.

Orangutan

A female has no hair on her face. A male has a beard.

WHERE IN THE WORLD?

LIVES: lowland rainforest, Borneo, Sumatra

EATS: mainly fruit, but also leaves, shoots and bird eggs

STATUS:
🔖 critically endangered

HOW BIG?

83–140cm (33–55in) long

Treetop giants
Long arms and legs help the orangutan swing. But it has to be careful, as it is the heaviest tree-dwelling animal in the world.

IN DANGER!

The orangutans' home is being destroyed for farming. In Borneo, a sanctuary rescues orphaned orangutans.

Jointed, flexible feet can be used like hands for eating.

IT'S WILD! While an orangutan builds a nest, it makes "raspberry" puffing noises.

WESTERN LOWLAND GORILLA

WHERE IN THE WORLD?

LIVES: lowland rainforest, Central Africa

EATS: roots, shoots, wild celery, tree bark and pulp

STATUS:
🍃 critically endangered

HOW BIG?

140–180cm
55–71in) long

When you watch a troop of gorillas, there's no question who's boss. The chief male, called a silverback, has shimmering silver back fur. When threatened, a silverback fights to keep his family safe. He leads a troop of up to thirty females and young.

A gorilla pulls faces and uses sign language to "talk" to other gorillas.

The silverback pounds his chest when he is angry.

It takes about eight years for a male's back fur to turn silver.

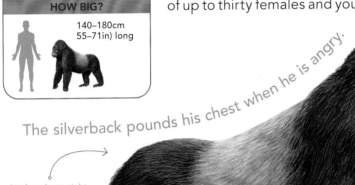

This ape's hands are similar to a human's. The thumbs help to grip objects.

Western lowland gorilla

The gorilla walks on its knuckles.

CHIMPANZEE

It's easy to find a troop of chimpanzees nearby because they are super noisy! When they sense danger, chimpanzees scream to scare off predators and to warn the others. Chimps are close relatives of us humans. They laugh, smile, hug each other, chatter and play, just like us.

A chimp has short thumbs, but long fingers, which are good for climbing.

SPOTTER FACT

At night, chimps make nests in trees. They fold over branches and tuck in leaves to make platforms.

Chimps teach their young to use tools.

WHERE IN THE WORLD?

LIVES: lowland rainforest, Central Africa

EATS: fruit, insects, leaves, seeds, bark, honey, pigs and even monkeys

STATUS:
endangered

HOW BIG?

100–160cm (39–63in) long

Helpful tools

Chimpanzees use tools. This chimp is poking a sharpened stick into a termites' nest to fish out the grubs to eat. Chimps also use stones to crack open nuts.

A chimp makes many calls. Its hoots, screams and grunts all carry different messages.

A chimp's feet are more like hands that can grip and hold.

Chimpanzee

IN DANGER

Chimpanzees are in danger because their homes are being destroyed. Forests are cut down for farming and mining.

Thick black-blue fur covers a chimp's body, except for the face, hands, feet and ears.

BONOBO

Don't confuse a bonobo with a chimpanzee even though they look similar. If you watch carefully, it's easy to tell the difference. A bonobo is calm and friendly, while a chimp fights and is noisy.

WHERE IN THE WORLD?

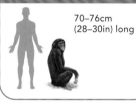

LIVES: lowland rainforest, Central Africa

EATS: fruit, leaves, honey, eggs and occasionally small insects

STATUS:
🌿 endangered

HOW BIG?

70–76cm (28–30in) long

Long fingers are good for gripping trees and grooming.

A male bonobo baby will stay with its mother's troop for life. An adult female may find another.

Bonobo

A bonobo can walk on all fours or upright, like us.

DON'T MISS!

Look for bonobos eating together. They often hunt, then share their food with the rest of the troop.

Piggyback

A mother feeds her new baby. She looks after and carries her baby around until it is about five years old.

IT'S WILD! When a bonobo becomes sick, it eats special leaves as medicine.

SUN BEAR

Because of the sun bear's name, you might be surprised to see this shy bear roaming the forest at night. The sun bear is the smallest member of the bear family and lives high in the trees.

WHERE IN THE WORLD?

LIVES: lowland rainforest, Southeast Asia

EATS: plants, seeds, fruit, beetles, honey, ants and termites

STATUS:
vulnerable

HOW BIG?

120–150cm (47–59in) long

SPOTTER FACT

A mother gives birth to one or two blind, helpless cubs. She cradles them in her arms like a human holds a baby.

An extremely long tongue laps up honey from bees' nests.

The sun bear is named for the bib of golden fur on its chest, which looks like the rising sun.

A short, glossy coat helps keep the sun bear cool in the heat and protects it against the rain.

Sun bear

IN DANGER

Sun bears are under threat. Their forest homes are being cut down for farmland.

Long claws rip into termite nests and grab the grubs to eat.

SLOTH BEAR

Noisy snorts and grunts let you know that a sloth bear is nearby. At night, this shaggy-coated, rather untidy-looking bear wanders the forest floor. The sloth bear loves to hunt for ants and termites.

WHERE IN THE WORLD?

LIVES: lowland rainforest and monsoon forest, India, Sri Lanka and Nepal

EATS: termites, ants, fruit, honey, beetles and grubs

STATUS:
vulnerable

HOW BIG?

140–190cm (55–75in) long

When a bear steals honey, thick fur protects it against angry bee stings.

The sloth bear's fur has no undercoat. This helps to keep the bear cool in the tropical heat.

SPOTTER FACT

A mother bear makes "bear's bread" for its young by vomiting up fruit and pieces of honeycomb.

The sloth bear sucks termites into its mouth through a gap in its front teeth.

Sharp claws rip into a rock-hard termites' nest.

Sloth bear

SOUTH AMERICAN COATI

Keep an ear out for the chatty babble of coatis. Coatis grunt, whistle and bark to one another as they hunt for grubs on the ground. If one coati sees a predator, it makes an alarm call and the rest of the band runs in all directions, stripy tails behind them.

DON'T MISS!

At night, coatis sleep in trees. A mother makes a comfy nest with leaves and twigs for her babies.

WHERE IN THE WORLD?

LIVES: lowland rainforest, northern South America, Central America and southwest USA

EATS: fruit, insects, lizards, small mammals, birds and bird and crocodile eggs

STATUS:
🌿 least concern

HOW BIG?

43–67cm (17–26in) long

South American coati

The coati's long snout pokes around under piles of leaves on the forest floor.

On the ground, a coati hunts for insects and grubs. In the trees, it eats fruit.

A coati uses its tail to help it balance on a tree branch.

IT'S WILD! Coatis are excellent climbers. Their flexible ankles mean they can climb down trees headfirst!

WHERE IN THE WORLD?

LIVES: lowland rainforest and mangrove forest, India

EATS: deer, wild boar, leopards, bears, water buffalo, porcupines, foxes, hares, birds and snakes

STATUS:
🌿 endangered

HOW BIG?

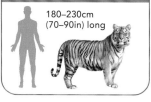

180–230cm (70–90in) long

BENGAL TIGER

A tiger can stalk so quietly that its prey doesn't know the tiger is there until it pounces. It has soft pads on the bottom of its feet that help it make no sound. It can run super fast and leap huge distances. A tiger can even swim well. No large mammal is safe when a hungry tiger is about!

IN DANGER!

Tigers are endangered. There are now more tigers in zoos than there are in the wild.

A tiger needs to eat only once a week, but it can eat the the equivalent of 240 burgers in one meal!

No two tigers have the same pattern of stripes.

The tiger is the world's largest big cat.

Bengal tiger

Powerful legs help to spring on unsuspecting prey.

JAGUAR

You'll be lucky to spot a jaguar, which is seldom seen. This big, nimble cat is an expert tree climber. A jaguar can even hang upside down below a large branch, with the help of its huge paws and strong, sharp claws.

To mark territory, a jaguar scratches trees with its sharp claws.

SPOTTER FACT

You can tell a jaguar from a leopard because the jaguar has spots within their spots. They have spotty spots!

Tree climber

A jaguar lives and hunts alone. It is an excellent swimmer as well as a good climber. A tree trunk is a perfect place to rest between hunts.

Powerful muscles help the jaguar to run super fast and jump huge lengths.

Jaguar

WHERE IN THE WORLD?

LIVES: lowland rainforest, Mexico, Central and South America

EATS: deer, monkeys, capybaras, tapirs, fish, turtles, armadillos, frogs, coatis and caimans

STATUS:
near threatened

HOW BIG?

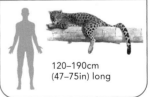

120–190cm
(47–75in) long

A jaguar's roar sounds like a deep, chesty cough.

WHERE IN THE WORLD?

LIVES: lowland rainforest and monsoon forest, Africa, Central Asia, India and China

EATS: gazelles, jackals, baboons, storks, rodents, reptiles and fish

STATUS: vulnerable

HOW BIG?

100–190cm (39–75in) long

LEOPARD

As the sun goes down, a leopard sets out to hunt. The leopard crouches low in the undergrowth, perfectly camouflaged in its surroundings, ready to pounce on unsuspecting prey. You might also see this agile cat in the branches above, dragging a large kill up a tree to save for later.

The leopard's spots are called rosettes because they are shaped like roses.

A leopard lives and hunts alone.

The leopard's strong legs could leap over three adult people lying head to toe.

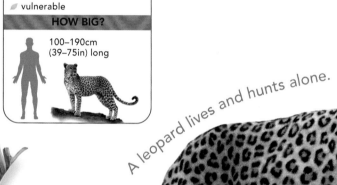

Leopard

A leopard can drag a kill three times its own weight up a tree.

SPOTTER FACT

A leopard can have a black coat, which still has rosettes, but they are dark and difficult to see.

CLOUDED LEOPARD

You'll be lucky to see the nimble clouded leopard. It is seldom seen and a bit mysterious. This amazing climber has huge paws with such strong, sharp claws that it can hang upside down below large branches!

LIVES: lowland rainforest and mangrove forest, mainland Southeast Asia and China

EATS: gibbons, macaques, deer, wild boar, rodents and birds

STATUS: vulnerable

HOW BIG?

68–106cm (27–42in) long

IN DANGER

The clouded leopard is hunted for its beautiful coat. In many countries, it is now illegal to kill clouded leopards.

The clouded leopard is named because of the huge, cloudlike spots on its fur.

The thick tail helps the leopard to balance while climbing trees.

Like most leopards, these cats live alone.

Clouded leopard

The clouded leopard lies in wait in trees, then ambushes its prey by leaping on it from above.

IT'S WILD The clouded leopard has the same-sized tearing teeth as a tiger, even though it is half its body size.

OCELOT

Take time to study the ocelot's beautiful coat with its swirls of spots and stripes splashing against golden fur. The ocelot hunts on the ground and up in the trees at night. By day it sleeps in high branches.

Strong legs help the ocelot to spring through the trees to catch its prey.

Climbing cat
The ocelot is an excellent climber. It leaps up into the trees to catch monkeys and birds.

An ocelot doesn't chew – it tears meat and swallows it whole.

An ocelot is twice the size of a pet cat.

Ocelot

WHERE IN THE WORLD?

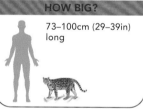

LIVES: lowland rainforest, southwest USA, Mexico, Central America and northern South America

EATS: rabbits, rodents, iguanas, fish and frogs

STATUS: least concern

HOW BIG?

73–100cm (29–39in) long

The ocelot's rough, scratchy tongue can lick a bone clean.

Mottled fur perfectly camouflages the ocelot in trees or in the undergrowth.

DON'T MISS!
Watch an ocelot in water. Unlike many cats, it is a great swimmer and can even catch fish.

IT'S WILD! Ocelots have been seen to go back to the same spot to poop. Avoid an ocelot toilet!

A fishing cat pounces on a flapping fish.

Water diet
The fishing cat eats frogs, water insects, and crayfish as well as fish. Its favorite way to hunt is from the water's edge.

FISHING CAT

Listen for splashes. The stocky fishing cat hunts in jungle rivers. First it gently taps the water to make the fish come to the surface, then, in a flash, it pounces! It scoops up the fish with its large paws or dives in to catch it headfirst.

The cat has an underlayer of fur that is short and waterproof.

The top layer of fur is longer and keeps the cat warm.

WHERE IN THE WORLD?

LIVES: lowland rainforest mangrove and monsoon forest, India

EATS: fish, crayfish, birds, insects and small rodents

STATUS:
vulnerable

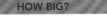
HOW BIG?

57–115cm (22–45in) long

DON'T MISS!
Keep watch. The fishing cat sometimes dives underwater, swimming up to grab a water bird from below.

Unusual webbed feet help the fishing cat to swim and walk in mud.

Fishing cat

ASIAN ELEPHANT

SPOTTER FACT

Elephants talk to each other with low rumbles that can be heard across the forest.

Is the earth shaking? No, a herd of Asian elephants is on the move, their feet thumping across the ground. They live in small groups of six or seven animals with a female in charge.

WHERE IN THE WORLD?

LIVES: lowland rainforest, India and Southeast Asia

EATS: fruits, trees and grasses

STATUS: endangered

HOW BIG?

5.5–6.6m (18–22ft) long

The trunk is used to smell, breathe, trumpet, drink, grab and spray other elephants.

An Asian elephant has smaller ears than an African one.

When an elephant lifts its tail, it means danger.

Asian elephant

The elephant sprays itself with dust to protect its skin from the sun.

IT'S WILD! Elephants have to eat for between twelve and eighteen hours a day to grow to their enormous size!

AFRICAN FOREST ELEPHANT

Meet the "mega-gardener" of the jungle. Every day, for up to eighteen hours, the African forest elephant eats leaves, seeds and fruits. When it poops, its fertile dung is full of seeds that help new plants and trees to grow.

WHERE IN THE WORLD?

LIVES: lowland rainforest, West Africa

EATS: tree bark, seeds, leaves, fruits

STATUS:
◢ endangered

HOW BIG?

1–3m (3–10ft) long

IN DANGER

Poachers hunt and kill elephants for their tusks. Antipoaching teams try to stop the hunters.

The African elephant flaps its huge ears to keep cool and to show how it feels.

African forest elephant

Two "fingers" at the end of the trunk grab and pick up objects.

The elephant uses its tusks to strip bark off trees to eat.

A baby elephant can walk the day it is born.

WEST INDIAN MANATEE

Don't mistake a manatee for a swimming elephant! This huge mammal is also called a "sea cow" because it grazes on seagrasses. When a manatee isn't eating, it spends about twelve hours a day resting, floating on or near the sea floor. The West Indian manatee has no natural predators, so it is safe while it naps.

WHERE IN THE WORLD?

LIVES: mangrove forest, coasts of southern USA, Central America, northern South America and the Caribbean

EATS: seagrass, mangrove leaves and algae

STATUS: vulnerable

HOW BIG?

3m (10ft) long

The manatee can hold its breath underwater for twenty minutes.

A manatee spends up to seven hours a day eating vast amounts of water plants.

The West Indian manatee lives in warm seas.

IN DANGER

The biggest dangers to manatees are boats, which cruise in warm waters and crash into these huge mammals.

The manatee uses its flippers to pass food to its lips.

West Indian manatee

AMAZONIAN MANATEE

Row silently down the Amazon River, and you may see the shy Amazonian manatee. Look for a nose poking out of the murky water. There aren't many plants to eat under the water, so the manatee surfaces to nibble grasses and water hyacinths floating on the top.

WHERE IN THE WORLD?

LIVES: lowland rainforest, the Amazon river basin, northern South America

EATS: water plants, seagrasses, water lilies and water hyacinths

STATUS: vulnerable

HOW BIG?

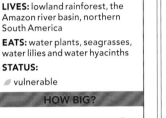

2.8m (9ft) long

This is the only manatee to live in freshwater rivers.

The manatee has whiskers that can sense movement.

A huge tail acts as a paddle to push the manatee along underwater.

The manatee's smooth body is buoyant, which means it floats easily.

DON'T MISS!

Look for manatee acrobatics. Manatees flip and roll together. They can even swim upside down.

Amazonian manatee

BRAZILIAN TAPIR

You will need excellent eyesight and lots of patience to spot the shy tapir in the dark, leafy undergrowth. A tapir lives alone unless it has a baby. At night, while the mother is off foraging, a young tapir's mottled, stripy coat helps it to hide on the forest floor. By the time the baby is one year old, it has a coat the same color as its mother. The baby is now ready to leave and live alone.

SPOTTER FACT

A tapir is a good swimmer. Often, it sinks underwater with only its snout above the water, just like a snorkel.

WHERE IN THE WORLD?

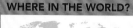

LIVES: lowland rainforest, northern South America

EATS: leaves, buds, twigs, fruit, grasses and water plants

STATUS:
🍃 vulnerable

HOW BIG?

2m (6.5ft) long

A tapir may look stocky, but it can run fast when escaping from caimans or jaguars!

A flexible snout can grasp leaves and shoots.

A young tapir is safest when it is close to its mother.

The tapir has wide feet that help it to walk across soggy ground.

Brazilian tapir

IT'S WILD! Tapirs are related to horses and rhinos.

MALAYAN TAPIR

It is dusk. Look carefully at the pools of shadows that make moving patterns on the forest floor. You might glimpse a Malayan tapir, with its black-and-white coat blending into the dappled light. Keep still and quiet or it might dive into the river. Once it's in, it closes its nostrils and sinks to avoid danger.

DON'T MISS!

Watch for a tapir pooping in water. It does this to stop a predator being able to follow its scent on land.

WHERE IN THE WORLD?

LIVES: lowland rainforest, Malaysia, Sumatra, Thailand and Myanmar

EATS: tender shoots and leaves, fruits, grasses and water plants

STATUS:
endangered

HOW BIG?

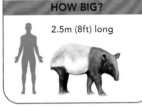

2.5m (8ft) long

The black-and-white colors break up the shape of the animal to camouflage it at night.

Malayan tapir

Tapirs do not see very well, but their senses of smell and hearing are excellent.

A Malayan tapir has the longest snout of any tapir.

SUMATRAN RHINO

WHERE IN THE WORLD?

LIVES: lowland rainforest, Indonesia

EATS: young saplings, leaves, twigs and shoots

STATUS:

✐ critically endangered

HOW BIG?

2.5–2.8m (8–9ft) long

It is extremely unlikely you will see a Sumatran rhino in the wild, because they are very rare. This kind of rhino lives alone. There are now fewer than eighty left in the wild, so they rarely come across each other to breed. Sadly, these rhinos are likely to become extinct.

IN DANGER

Rhinos are hunted for their horns. Even though this rhino has small horns, it is still hunted for them.

Hairy skin helps to cake mud onto the rhino's body to keep it cool.

The Sumatran rhino has two horns, but one is no more than a bump.

Sumatran rhinos talk to each other by whining, whistling and kicking around their dung!

Sumatran rhino

IT'S WILD! To help save the Sumatran rhino, conservationists are trying to breed them in captivity.

CHEVROTAINS

You might need to wait a long time to spot one of these tiny, shy animals, also known as mouse deer. Chevrotains are rare. They are not actually deer—chevrotains are in their own animal family. They spend their days hiding from predators on the jungle floor.

WHERE IN THE WORLD?

LIVES: lowland rainforest
- Water chevrotain, West Africa
- Greater Malay chevrotain, Malaysia and Indonesia
- Lesser Malay chevrotain, Southeast Asia, China

EATS: fallen fruit, water plants, buds, leaves, grasses and fungi

STATUS:
least concern

HOW BIG?

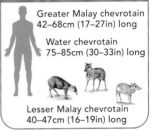

Greater Malay chevrotain 42–68cm (17–27in) long

Water chevrotain 75–85cm (30–33in) long

Lesser Malay chevrotain 40–47cm (16–19in) long

A water chevrotain can hold its breath underwater for five minutes.

Water chevrotain

To communicate, the chevrotain stamps its hooves fast to sound like a drum roll.

SPOTTER FACT

Chevrotains have not changed much in the millions of years they have lived on Earth.

Lesser Malay chevrotain

Take a close look at the mouth of the Lesser Malay chevrotain. It has fangs.

Greater Malay chevrotain

IT'S WILD! The silver-backed chevrotain was not seen for 30 years and thought to be extinct. It was rediscovered in 2019!

ZEBRA DUIKER

The best way to spot a zebra duiker is to look for other animals munching in the trees. The duiker waits on the forest floor to pick up any fruit or nuts that are dropped from above. But you'll have to look carefully—the duiker's stripes keep it hidden among the shadowy trees.

DON'T MISS!

You might see a zebra duiker cracking open fruit and nuts with its hard, bony head!

The zebra duiker is so small, it is sometimes taken by birds of prey.

A zebra duiker lives alone except when it has babies to look after.

Zebra duiker

Thin legs help the duiker to trot through dense forest.

WHERE IN THE WORLD?

LIVES: lowland rainforest, West Africa

EATS: fruit, leaves, grasses and nuts

STATUS:
vulnerable

HOW BIG?

90cm (35in) long

PYGMY HIPPOPOTAMUS

During the day, a pygmy hippopotamus hides and snoozes in the swampy water. You are more likely to spot one at night when it comes out onto the river bank, hungry for food. The pygmy hippopotamus returns to the water in the heat of the day because if it spends too much time on land, its skin will dry out.

WHERE IN THE WORLD?

LIVES: lowland rainforest, West Africa

EATS: leaves, roots, ferns and fruits

STATUS: endangered

HOW BIG?

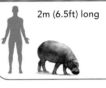

2m (6.5ft) long

The pygmy hippo's sweat contains natural sunscreen to stop the hippo getting sunburnt.

The hippo's skin is greenish-black, getting lighter as it reaches its belly.

The hippo's ears and nostrils close while swimming.

Thick feet help the hippo to walk along riverbeds.

Pygmy hippopotamus

CAPYBARA

SPOTTER FACT

In the morning, a capybara eats its own poop, which is full of protein. This helps to digest the grass it eats.

Scan the river carefully and you may see the largest rodent in the world. Look for the capybara's nose, eyes and ears peeking above the water. It stays alert for jaguars, anacondas and birds on the hunt. If scared, it dives underwater.

WHERE IN THE WORLD?

LIVES: lowland rainforest, northern and central South America

EATS: grasses, aquatic plants, fruit and tree bark

STATUS:

🍃 least concern

HOW BIG?

100–130cm (39–51in) long

A capybara can stay underwater for up to five minutes.

A capybara's teeth never stop growing. Chewing helps to keep them worn down.

Reddish dark-brown fur is long and thin and dries out quickly after swimming.

Capybara

Webbed feet help the capybara to paddle through the water.

On the lookout
A capybara's eyes, nose and ears are high up on its head so that the rest of its body can be hidden underwater.

IT'S WILD! Sometimes capybaras nap in the water, floating at the surface.

BICOLOR-SPINED PORCUPINE

Watch out! This bicolor-spined porcupine has sharp spines all over its body, except for its long tail. This rodent lives in the middle layer of the rainforest, climbing trees and eating fruit and leaves. It rarely reaches the forest floor.

WHERE IN THE WORLD?

LIVES: lowland rainforest, western South America

EATS: leaves and fruit

STATUS:

🍃 least concern

HOW BIG?

43–81cm (17–32in) long

The sharp spines are yellow near the skin and tipped with black.

SPOTTER FACT

If you see this porcupine standing on its back legs, shaking its spines, it's ready to attack!

The porcupine is slow-moving, but nothing much attacks it, with all those spines!

DON'T MISS!

Look for the porcupine in a ball shape. It rolls up and pushes its spines out to protect its body from a predator.

The strong tail wraps and grips around branches and twigs.

The tail is almost the same length as the body.

Bicolor-spined porcupine

IT'S WILD! The bicolor-spined porcupine moans, grunts, coughs, shrieks, and even barks.

LOWLAND PACA

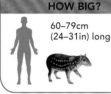
The time to spot a paca is in the dark of night. During the day it hides deep underground in a burrow, which has two entrances covered in leaves. If the leaves of one entrance are disturbed, the paca knows a predator is nearby. It's time to run out of the other entrance!

SPOTTER FACT

A male and female paca stay together for life to raise babies, but live separately. Each has its own burrow.

Three to five lines of spots lie along the paca's back.

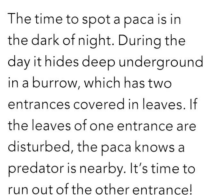

Sharp claws dig burrows to sleep in.

The paca uses its claws to climb trees in search of fruit.

Lowland paca

AGOUTIS

Keep your eyes peeled for an agouti making a fast getaway from a snake or eagle. The agouti can run, jump and even swim fast! Its hairy skin is covered in a stinky oily coating that makes it waterproof.

SPOTTER FACT

Agoutis eat Brazil nuts, which drop to the ground. An agouti cracks the nut open with its sharp front teeth.

Red agouti

Brazilian agouti

An agouti buries nuts to eat later. Some of the nuts grow into new trees.

To show it is cross, the agouti raises its bottom and fluffs out the long hair on its rump!

WHERE IN THE WORLD?

LIVES: lowland rainforest

● Red agouti, northern South America

◉ Brazilian agouti, Brazil

○ Gray agouti, western South America

EATS: fruit, nuts and seeds

STATUS:

🍃 all least concern

HOW BIG?

42–62cm (17–24in) long

Gray agouti

The agouti's back feet have three toes with claws that look similar to hoofs.

LIVES: lowland rainforest and monsoon forest, eastern Australia and Tasmania

EATS: worms, insect larvae, fish, freshwater shrimp and crayfish

STATUS:

🔖 near threatened

HOW BIG?

38–60cm
(15–24in) long

PLATYPUS

Point your binoculars toward the riverbank, and prepare to see an unusual animal. This mammal has a bill and webbed feet like a duck. It swims like an otter, and, really unusually, the platypus lays eggs.

Furry egg-layer
When the platypus babies hatch from their eggs, the mother feeds her young by sweating milk out of her stomach.

A broad, flat tail allows the platypus to move through the water.

Dense, waterproof fur keeps the platypus warm in water.

The bill senses food and helps to steer in the water, too.

SPOTTER FACT
The platypus is one of the few poisonous mammals. It can inject poison though its back claws.

Platypus

ECHIDNAS

Look for a spiny bottom poking above the ground. When the echidna senses danger, it digs straight down so only its bottom shows, spines upright. The echidna is the only mammal, apart from the platypus, that lays eggs.

SPOTTER'S FACT

A female lays a tiny egg and rolls it into a pouch on her belly. The egg hatches and the baby grows in the pouch.

The echidna's feet are curved backward to help when digging.

The echidna has a long, sticky tongue that laps up ants and termites.

Long-nosed echidna

The world's largest flea lives on the echidna.

The spines are actually thick, sharp hairs.

WHERE IN THE WORLD?

LIVES: lowland rainforest and monsoon forest
- ◉ long-nosed echidna, New Guinea
- ◉ short-nosed echidna, Australia, New Guinea and Papua New Guinea

EATS: ants, termites, worms and grubs

STATUS:
- ◢ long-nosed echidna – critically endangered
- ◢ short-nosed echidna – least concern

HOW BIG?

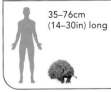

35–76cm (14–30in) long

Short-nosed echidna

IT'S WILD A baby echidna is called a puggle. When it is born, it doesn't have spines.

COMMON SPOTTED CUSCUS

In the daytime, you'll need to search hard for the common spotted cuscus. To keep out of sight from hungry eagles and pythons, the cuscus tucks its head between its legs and pulls a blanket of leaves over itself. But if anything tries to take over its eating spot, it will hiss and attack.

SPOTTER FACT

The cuscus is a marsupial. Like a kangaroo, it has a pouch where it keeps its baby.

WHERE IN THE WORLD?

LIVES: lowland rainforest, Australia, New Guinea

EATS: plants, leaves, flowers

STATUS:
🌿 least concern

HOW BIG?

35–65cm (14–26in) long

Look for the cuscus' orange eyes.

The cuscus is sometimes called the "monkey marsupial."

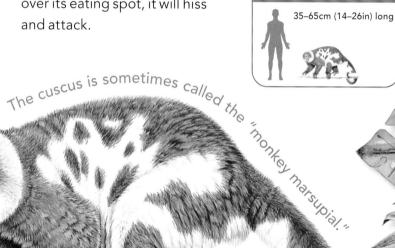

Common spotted cuscus

Sharp claws are excellent for climbing as well as for grooming fur.

The tail curls around and grips branches to help climbing.

IT'S WILD! The common spotted cuscus marks its territory with a stinky scent.

POSSUMS

It's an inky-black night in the jungle. Can you make out the shadowy shapes of possums in the trees? As they climb, they coil their long tails around branches for balance. The possums grasp the wet, slippery bark with sharp claws.

Possums are marsupials. They have a pouch to hold their young.

Herbert River ringtail possum

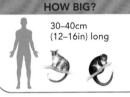
Common ringtail possum

A possum's strong tail helps it to hang onto branches. It can even hang upside down by its tail!

SPOTTER FACT
When a possum is threatened, it keeps still and plays dead. Many predators like to eat animals that are alive.

A gap between the second and third fingers helps it grip around branches.

GOODFELLOW'S TREE KANGAROO

If you happen to spot a Goodfellow's tree kangaroo on the ground, notice how it moves slowly and clumsily. But up in the trees, it sprints like an athlete. It can jump up to roughly the height of a two-story building!

In hot weather, the tree kangaroo licks itself to keep cool.

To climb, this kangaroo's arms cling to a branch and its hind legs bounce up behind it.

Goodfellow's tree kangaroo

SPOTTER FACT

The tree kangaroo is a marsupial. The mother gives birth to a baby, which climbs into a pouch. It stays there for a year.

Look for the two golden stripes that run down the back to the tail.

A long tail helps the tree kangaroo to balance while climbing.

WHERE IN THE WORLD?

LIVES: lowland rainforest, New Guinea and Papua New Guinea

EATS: mainly the leaves of the silkwood tree, but also fruit, flowers and grasses

STATUS: endangered

HOW BIG?

58–78cm (23–31in) long

IT'S WILD! The tree kangaroo sleeps after eating. It sleeps for more than half of the day.

BENNETT'S TREE KANGAROO

When it rains heavily, a Bennett's tree kangaroo takes shelter in thick layers of leaves in the middle of the trees. When it drizzles, it's easier to spot one near the edges of the branches. Under clear skies, watch this marsupial sunbathing at the top of the canopy.

WHERE IN THE WORLD?

LIVES: lowland rainforest, northeastern Australia

EATS: trees, leaves and fruit

STATUS:
near threatened

HOW BIG?

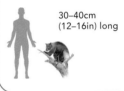

30–40cm
(12–16in) long

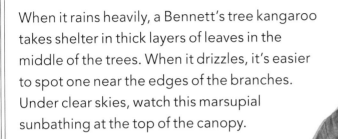

Dark fur on the face and stomach camouflage the kangaroo from animals below.

Bennett's tree kangaroo

DON'T MISS!
Watch out if you stand below a tree. The tree kangaroo sometimes drops to the ground suddenly!

SPOTTER FACT
A Bennett's tree kangaroo hops rather than runs along a tree branch. It uses its tail for extra balance.

The baby leaves the pouch at one year old, but continues to jump back in if it feels scared.

IT'S WILD! Tree kangaroos have rubbery soles on their hands and feet that grip onto branches.

BIRDS

HOW TO SPOT BIRDS

Look up to see a flock of brightly colored parrots dart through the treetops, while a green kakapo pecks for seeds on the forest floor. Birds come in many different shapes and sizes and, with their colorful feathers and beaks, are easy to recognize.

Follow the sound
The hornbill makes a barking sound that echoes through the trees.

Study the beak
The shape of a bird's beak helps it to grab and eat different types of food. The hornbill uses its long beak to reach for fruit.

WHAT MAKES A BIRD?

FEATHERS A bird's body is covered with a light, tough layer of feathers.

WINGS All birds have wings. Most of them use their wings to fly.

EGGS Birds hatch from eggs. Many birds build nests for their young.

BEAKS A bird does not have teeth. It has a hornlike bill or beak.

WARM-BLOODED A bird is warm-blooded, which means it keeps its body at the same warm temperature no matter how hot or cold its surroundings.

VERTEBRATE A bird is a vertebrate, which means it has a backbone.

Notice a bird's shape
When a hornbill perches, its tail feathers drop beneath its feet.

Look up and listen
From dawn to dusk, listen for jungle birds hooting, squawking, and singing to each other. Study a bird's shape and color so you can identify it quickly—it may not stay still for long.

Great hornbill

Plan when to go
During the day, hornbills fly in small groups searching for food. At dusk, they settle down high up in the trees for the night.

Bodies for flying

Parrots have long tail feathers and shorter wing feathers to help steer and dive through tightly packed trees.

Where do birds live?

Most birds can fly, which means many nest and search for food in the canopy, at the top of the trees. Some birds prefer to find food and stay safe in the dark lower branches.

BIRD WATCH

Imagine making a study of just one rainforest tree from first light until nightfall. Which birds come and go? What do they eat? Who's nesting where? Before a trip, research the birds you expect to see.

Bills for feeding

Jungle birds have beaks to help them feed from particular plants. The hummingbird's long beak can reach deep into a flower to sip nectar.

Feathers for camouflage

A kakapo cannot fly. Its green and brown feathers help to keep it unseen on the ground, safe from predators.

CASSOWARY

The casque

Head down, a cassowary dips its beak and pelts through the forest. This bird cannot fly but is a fast runner and swimmer. Look for the male, who takes care of the chicks. He's less brightly colored than the female. Both the male and the female have a bony horn on their head called a casque.

Chin skin
A cassowary has brightly colored folds of skin under its chin called a wattle. The wattle becomes brighter in color when the bird is agitated.

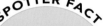

SPOTTER FACT

The cassowary is able to eat a plum that is poisonous to all other animals. It is known as the cassowary plum.

No one knows what the casque is for, but it might make its call louder.

Stiff, bristly feathers keep the bird dry and protect its skin from thorns.

WHERE IN THE WORLD?

LIVES: lowland rainforest and mangrove forest, eastern Indonesia, Papua New Guinea, northeastern Australia

EATS: fallen fruit, fungi, insects, small invertebrates

STATUS:
least concern

HOW BIG?

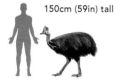

150cm (59in) tall

Feet with three sharp dagger-type toes attack predators.

Cassowary

GREAT CURASSOW

Splat! Ripe fruit falls from a tree, ready for this slender bird to scoop up in its sturdy beak. Look for groups of great curassows foraging for food on the forest floor.

IN DANGER

Great curassows' numbers are dropping fast because the rainforest is being cut down for farming.

A male has a yellow knob on its beak.

The male has a booming call, made louder through a long windpipe.

Dark plumage camouflages the great curassow on the forest floor.

Great curassow

The great curassow has long legs to find food on the ground and escape danger.

WHERE IN THE WORLD?

LIVES: lowland rainforest, Mexico, Central America, western Colombia, northwestern Ecuador

EATS: fruit, berries, seeds and invertebrates

STATUS:
vulnerable

HOW BIG?

80–100cm (31–39in) long

INDIAN PEAFOWL

What a spectacle! The male peacock raises his tail feathers into a huge, green-blue feathery fan. The feathers have beautiful markings that look like hundreds of eyes. The peacock dances around trying to impress the female peahen. If you listen, you can hear the drumlike rattle as he flutters and shakes his feathers to catch her attention.

SPOTTER FACT

If a peacock's feather is grabbed by a predator, it falls out easily.

The feathers are iridescent, which means they shimmer in the light.

It is thought that the female chooses the male based on the size, color and quality of his tail fan.

When the peacock walks or flies, it folds his tail down and drags it behind its body.

Indian peacock

The male grows
a new set of
feathers each year.

WHERE IN THE WORLD?

LIVES: monsoon forest, India
and Sri Lanka

EATS: seeds, insects, fruit,
small mammals, reptiles

STATUS:

🌿 least concern

HOW BIG?

100–115cm
(39–45in) long,
not including tail

Indian peahen

CONGO SERPENT EAGLE

Keep a sharp eye out in the shadowy understory for the Congo serpent eagle. It sits on a low branch watching for a snake or lizard on the dark forest floor. Then suddenly, the eagle drops down on top of the prey from above. It snatches the prey in its sharp claws.

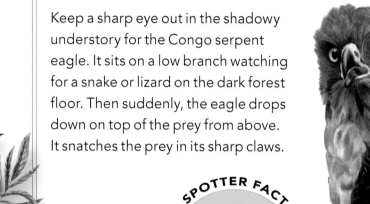

This eagle can see twice as well as a human.

Dark feathers hide the serpent eagle from prey.

Short wings help the eagle to dart quickly through the trees.

The Congo serpent eagle has a long, rounded tail.

Super-sharp claws tear into prey.

Congo serpent eagle

SPOTTER FACT

The Congo serpent eagle is one of the noisiest birds of prey. It makes a meowing and, a "cow-cow-cow" noise.

WHERE IN THE WORLD?

LIVES: lowland rainforest, West and Central Africa

EATS: snakes, lizards, toads, small mammals

STATUS:

◢ least concern

HOW BIG?

50–60cm (20–24in) long

PHILIPPINE EAGLE

The Philippine eagle is also known as the "monkey-eating eagle." It perches high up in a tree, waiting until the timing is just right, then plunges to catch a monkey in the branches below. The eagle grips its prey with powerful, bone-crushing claws and flies off.

WHERE IN THE WORLD?

LIVES: lowland rainforest, the Philippines

EATS: monkeys and other mammals, birds and reptiles

STATUS:
🍃 critically endangered

HOW BIG?

86–102cm (34–40in) long

Slender wing feathers help the eagle to swoop at speed.

Long, brown feathers form a shaggy crest.

Huge talons pierce and grip onto prey.

Philippine eagle

DON'T MISS!

See a young eagle learning to fly. It practices by jumping between branches while flapping its wings.

DON'T MISS!

Look for a chick climbing a tree, gripping with its beak, feet and special claws on its wings.

Locals call the hoatzin the "stink bird" because of its smelly breath!

The hoatzin is noisy. It makes croaks, groans, hisses and grunts to other birds.

If a chick falls into water, it can swim.

Hoatzin

The hoatzin spends much of the day perched on a branch, munching leaves.

WHERE IN THE WORLD?

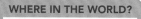

LIVES: lowland rainforest, northern South America

EATS: leaves and occasionally fruit, flowers

STATUS:
🍃 least concern

HOW BIG?

60cm (24in) long

HOATZIN

Do you think the spiky-crested hoatzin looks as if it's from prehistoric times? It's noisy and stinks, too. When the hoatzin spreads its wings, it croaks and hisses. It smells foul because of the way it digests its food. It has a pouch where the leaves it eats ferment, or ripen.

IT'S WILD! A hoatzin is not that good at flying. It flies short distances clumsily.

SUNBITTERN

Point your binoculars onto the river shoreline to see a sunbittern wading in the shallows. If you see something frighten the bird, in a second, it will fan open its huge wings to show large spots that look just like eyes.

WHERE IN THE WORLD?

LIVES: lowland rainforest, northern South America

EATS: insects, crabs, spiders, shrimp, fish, frogs, lizards and earthworms

STATUS:
least concern

HOW BIG?

48cm (19in) long

Sunny red and orange feathers give this bird its name.

When the sunbittern spreads its wings in defense, it also hisses.

A long beak spears fish in the forest rivers.

SPOTTER FACT

If a predator threatens the nest of chicks, one parent will pretend it has broken a wing to distract the predator.

Sunbittern

IT'S WILD! A sunbittern sometimes wiggles a worm in the water as a lure to catch a fish.

VICTORIA CROWNED PIGEON

Watch as a male Victoria crowned pigeon puts on a dancing show to attract a mate. First he bobs his white-tipped head crest, then he stretches forward and swings his head up and down. All the while, he wags his tail.

Both the male and the female have a crest.

DON'T MISS!

The Victoria crowned pigeon was named after the British Queen Victoria.

This pigeon rarely flies, but can flap onto a branch to escape danger.

Look for the striking red eyes.

WHERE IN THE WORLD?

LIVES: lowland rainforest, Indonesia and Papua New Guinea

EATS: fruit, seeds, berries and small invertebrates

STATUS:
near threatened

HOW BIG?

76cm (30in) long

On the ground, the pigeon lollops along with a rolling walk.

Victoria crowned pigeon

NICOBAR PIGEON

WHERE IN THE WORLD?

The Nicobar pigeon is the closest living relative to the dodo, which died out more than 400 years ago. The Nicobar pigeon is now also very rare. Zoos help keep these birds safe so they can breed, or have young.

LIVES: lowland rainforest, Southeast Asia and Oceania

EATS: seeds, fruit, buds

STATUS:
near threatened

HOW BIG?

40cm (16in) long

Nicobar pigeon

The Nicobar pigeon has vibrant green feathers and a shaggy mane around its neck.

The tail is short and pure white.

SUPERB FRUIT DOVE

WHERE IN THE WORLD?

Listen for the sound of whistling from the sky. When a superb fruit dove flies, air passes over its wing feathers and makes a whistling noise. These birds make a steady "coo-coo" call to each other, too.

LIVES: lowland rainforest, Southeast Asia and Australasia

EATS: fruit

STATUS:
least concern

HOW BIG?

20–24cm (8–9in) long

Superb fruit dove

The dove's mouth can open wide to eat large fruit.

White-crowned parrot

The white-crowned parrot lives high up in the canopy.

This parrot feeds in flocks of up to fifty birds.

PARROTS

Parrots put on daredevil acrobatics shows, including hanging from branches with their feet and beaks. Many parrots are a brilliant bright green color. Different kinds of parrots have splashes of flaming-red, sunshine-yellow, and sky-blue feathers.

Look for the red strip on the tail of the male parrot.

This parrot is an excellent mimic. It copies lots of rainforest sounds.

WHERE IN THE WORLD?

LIVES: lowland rainforest

- White-crowned parrot, Central America and Mexico
- Hanging parrots, Southeast Asia and Pacific Islands
- Blue-fronted parrot, South America
- Eclectus parrot, New Guinea and nearby islands, northeast Australia
- Buff-faced pygmy parrot, New Guinea

EATS: seeds, nuts, fruit

STATUS:
least concern

HOW BIG?

White-crowned parrot 24cm (9in) long

Hanging parrots 12-14cm (5-6in) long

Blue-fronted parrot 38cm (15in) long

Eclectus parrot 35cm (14in) long

Buff-faced pygmy parrot 8.5cm (3in) long

Blue-crowned hanging parrot

Vernal hanging parrot

SPOTTER FACT

Hanging parrots hang upside down to reach food to eat. They sometimes sleep upside down, too.

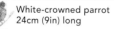
IT'S WILD! Parrots can make good pets, but many types are rare and should be left in the wild.

Pygmy parrots are the smallest parrots in the world.

Buff-faced pygmy parrot

SPOTTER FACT

A parrot is the only bird that is able to pick up food with its beak, then move the food to its mouth.

A female eclectus parrot is mostly bright red and purple.

The male eclectus parrot is a brilliant emerald-green color.

This parrot has an easily recognizable turquoise patch on its head.

The male and female eclectus parrots look so different that it was thought they were different species for a long itme.

Eclectus parrots

Gripping claws
Parrots grip branches with long, sharp claws. Two claws face forward and two face backward.

Blue-fronted parrot

IT'S WILD! Thousands of captive parrots have escaped into the wild in the UK. There are now 20,000 living there.

MACAWS

At dawn, look up to see brilliantly colored feathers flash through the treetops. Flocks of macaws take to the skies from their nests in search of a breakfast of nuts and seeds. Their loud squawks echo through the canopy.

A strong, curved beak has a sharp edge for crushing tough nuts.

Scarlet macaw

Long tail feathers help the macaw to fly fast and change direction.

WHERE IN THE WORLD?

LIVES: lowland rainforest
○ Scarlet macaw, Central America and South America

EATS: nuts, seeds and some eat small insects and fruit

STATUS:
◢ Scarlet macaw – least concern

HOW BIG?

Scarlet macaw 89cm (35in) long

IT'S WILD! To land, a macaw drops down its tail and feet, then brakes with its wings.

Kakapo concerts
This big parrot has a big voice. Its booming, high-pitched concerts can last for eight hours!

KAKAPO

You won't find a kakapo in the sky, because it can't fly. It's the heaviest parrot, so should be easy to spot on the ground, but its green and yellow feathers blend into the scrubby forest floor.

WHERE IN THE WORLD?

LIVES: lowland rainforest, some islands off the coast of New Zealand

EATS: seeds, leaves, fruit

STATUS:
🌿 critically endangered

HOW BIG?

🖐 64cm (25in) long

The kakapo has a musty, sweet smell that other kakapos recognize.

The kakapo's strong beak grinds up leaves and fruit.

IN DANGER!
There are only about 200 kakapos in the wild. Local people protect them in the hope that their numbers will rise.

The kakapo has hard feet and claws, which are used for walking and climbing.

Kakapo

PESQUET'S PARROT

How can you tell if a Pesquet's parrot is male or female? A male has a red spot behind each eye. Animal experts think this parrot doesn't have feathers on its face so it can keep clean when it eats sticky fig pulp.

This parrot makes loud screeching calls.

The beak is slightly hooked to tear into figs.

DON'T MISS!
Keep an eye out for a Pesquet's parrot flying overhead. It constantly switches between hard flapping and gliding.

Pesquet's parrot

This bird spends hours sitting on high branches in the forest.

WHERE IN THE WORLD?

LIVES: Lowland rainforest, New Guinea

EATS: figs, mangoes, sometimes flowers and nectar

STATUS: vulnerable

HOW BIG?

46cm (18in) long

RED-FAN PARROT

Turn your binoculars upward to see the red-fan parrot high in the canopy. Look near old trees, where it often builds a nest. Usually, a female lays one or two eggs inside a tree.

Feathered fan
The red-fan parrot puffs up its long neck feathers into a spectacular fan. This makes attackers think it's a much bigger bird.

WHERE IN THE WORLD?

LIVES: lowland rainforest, northern South America

EATS: fruit

STATUS:
🍃 least concern

HOW BIG?

36cm (14in) long

The head and curved beak are shaped like a hawk's – it is also known as the hawk-headed parrot.

The male and female have the same coloring and crest.

Red-fan parrot

Short tail feathers help the parrot to dart through the trees.

SPOTTER FACT
The red-fan parrot sways while making whistling and chattering sounds to attract a mate.

IT'S WILD! This is a rare bird that many bird watchers would love to spot.

SALMON-CRESTED COCKATOO

With its super-loud screech, you will definitely hear the salmon-crested cockatoo. If its headcrest is raised, the cockatoo is likely to be angry or afraid.

WHERE IN THE WORLD?

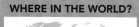

LIVES: lowland rainforest, Eastern Indonesia

EATS: seeds, nuts, fruit and insects

STATUS:
🍃 vulnerable

HOW BIG?

40–50cm (16–20in) long

The cockatoo sometimes raises its crest to attract a mate.

This cockatoo's beak is so powerful it can crack a coconut.

Look for a yellow tinge on the underwing.

This cockatoo is covered in pale pink feathers.

Salmon-crested cockatoo

IN DANGER
Many people are trying to protect these birds by stopping them from being sold as pets.

IT'S WILD! The Malay name for this bird is "kakaktua," which means "older sister" or "older brother."

JACAMARS

If you see a branch with jacamars on it, settle down for a treat. They feed by "hawking." The jacamars sit with their beaks tilted up and wait for insects to fly past. Then, quick as a flash, they shoot after flying butterflies or wasps and grab them in midair.

Jacamars go back to the same perch time and time again.

Watch the metallic-colored feathers shimmer in the sunlight.

Rufous-tailed jacamar

Paradise jacamar

WHERE IN THE WORLD?

LIVES: lowland rainforest
- ⊙ Paradise jacamar, northern South America
- ● Rufous-tailed jacamar, Central and northern South America

EATS: flying insects

STATUS:
least concern

HOW BIG?

Rufous-tailed jacamar 25cm (10in) long

Paradise jacamar 30cm (12in) long

RUFOUS WOODPECKER

WHERE IN THE WORLD?

LIVES: lowland rainforest, South and Southeast Asia

EATS: ants, termites, sap and nectar

STATUS:
least concern

HOW BIG?

25cm (10in) long

Look for an ants' nest and you might also find a pair of rufous woodpeckers. They love to eat ants and termites. These woodpeckers even build their nests in old anthills.

The black tips on the feathers make the woodpecker look stripy.

Rufous woodpecker

IT'S WILD! Ants spray predators with a stinky liquid in defense. The woodpecker sometimes smells of the ant spray.

TROGONS

If you go trogon spotting, look for a couple of tail feathers sticking out of a hole in a tree. The resplendent quetzal's tail is so long that when it is in its nest, its tail feathers hang out. Trogons gnaw holes in trees or termite mounds to make nests.

Short, strong wings fly for small distances, rather than long journeys.

Red-headed trogon

Look for the shimmering, metallic-looking tail feathers.

The male Narina trogon has a green throat, which puffs out when it hoots.

The long tail feathers of the resplendent quetzal are much longer than its body and hang far below a branch.

WHERE IN THE WORLD?

LIVES: lowland rainforest
- Resplendent quetzal, Central America
- Green-backed trogon, central and northwest South America
- Red-headed trogon, Southeast Asia
- Narina trogon, Central and southern Africa

EATS: fruit, invertebrates and reptiles

STATUS:
- Resplendent quetzal – near threatened
- other trogons – least concern

HOW BIG?

Resplendent quetzal 40cm (16in) long, (not including longer tail feathers)

Green-backed trogon 30cm (12in) long

Narina trogon 34cm (13in) long

Red-headed trogon 34cm (13in) long

DON'T MISS!

Trogon legs and feet are short and weak. Watch as the birds shuffle along a branch, using their wings to help.

Narina trogon

Resplendent quetzal

IT'S WILD! Fossils, or remains, of trogons have been found in Europe that show they lived 49 million years ago!

Spot this trogon early in the morning catching moths in the air while it flies.

This female green-backed trogon's tail has more stripes than the male's.

Green-backed trogon

GREAT BLUE TURACO

When the great blue turaco flies, it looks awkward and ungraceful. When it lands, it bumps along the ground. But this big bird is excellent at climbing. It spends most of its life in the trees.

The striking crest stands up at all times.

Great blue turaco

This bird leaps, rather than flies, from branch to branch.

WHERE IN THE WORLD?

LIVES: lowland rainforest, West, Central and East Africa

EATS: fruit, leaves, flowers, buds, shoots, insects

STATUS:
least concern

HOW BIG?

70–76cm (28–30in) long

A fourth toe rotates, or turns, to help with climbing.

The long tail helps this bird to balance.

TOCO TOUCAN

A flock of toucans flies high in the canopy, croaking loudly, just like a chorus of frogs. Toucans recognize each other from their loud squawks. Each type has its own call.

A toucan sleeps with its bill under its wing to keep warm.

A toucan's long bill is used to reach fruit on branches.

The bill has a jagged, sharp edge to peel fruit.

WHERE IN THE WORLD?

LIVES: lowland rainforest, central and eastern South America

EATS: fruit, insects, bird eggs, small reptiles, small amphibians

STATUS:
◣ least concern

HOW BIG?

55–65cm (22–26in) long

The toucan uses its feet to hop along branches.

Toco toucan

IT'S WILD The toucan's beak is not as heavy as it looks. It is filled with a light, spongy material.

GREAT HORNBILL

Look for a male hornbill pushing food through a hole in a tree. He's feeding his female mate, who is sitting on her eggs inside. The male blocks her inside the tree with mud. When the chicks are ready, she will come out from the nest.

The big lump on the beak is called a casque.

Unlike the toucan, the hornbill's beak is very heavy.

Great hornbill

Super-strong neck muscles hold the weight of the beak.

Large, sturdy wings are strong enough to keep this heavy bird in the air.

WHERE IN THE WORLD?

LIVES: lowland rainforest, Southeast Asia and the west coast of India

EATS: fruit, small mammals, birds, reptiles and insects

STATUS:
vulnerable

HOW BIG?

110–120cm (43–47in) long

DON'T MISS!

Listen for a flock of hornbills flying overhead. You can hear their heavy wingbeats from the ground.

The shining green throat feathers of this carib shine in the light.

Crimson topaz

The crossed tail feathers make this hummingbird easy to see.

Green-throated carib

SPOTTER FACT

The bee hummingbird is the smallest bird in the world. It's about the size of your thumb.

The female purple-throated carib has a curved beak.

SPOTTER FACT

Hummingbirds flap so fast that they can fly forward and backward and hover and can even fly upside down.

Purple-throated carib

Bee hummingbird

HUMMINGBIRDS

Hummingbirds live at the very tops of the trees where sweet-smelling flowers grow. As a hummingbird hovers, it flaps its wings so fast they look like a blur. A hummingbird dips its long beak into a bell-shaped flower and drinks up a syrupy juice, called nectar.

The sword-billed hummingbird is the only bird to have a beak longer than its body! It is used to reach inside long, tube-shaped flowers.

To hover, a hummingbird flaps its wings in a figure-of-eight shape.

The bee hummingbird visits up to 1,500 flowers a day.

A huge heart pumps blood to the wings so hummingbirds can flap fast.

Collared inca

This hummingbird flies high in the cloud forests of the Andes.

WHERE IN THE WORLD?

LIVES: lowland rainforest and monsoon forest

- Collared inca, South American Andes
- Sword-billed hummingbird, South American Andes
- Crimson topaz, northeastern South America
- Bee hummingbird, Cuba
- Purple-throated carib and green-throated carib, Caribbean

EATS: flower nectar, insects

STATUS:

- bee hummingbird – near threatened
- all other hummingbirds – least concern

HOW BIG?

Collared inca
10–14cm
(4–5.5in) long

Purple-throated carib
11–12cm (4.5in) long

Sword-billed
hummingbird 13–14cm
(5–5.5in) long

Crimson topaz
21–23cm (8–9in) long

Green-throated
carib 10–12cm
(4–4.5in) long

Bee hummingbird
5.5cm (2in) long

SPOTTER FACT

Hummingbirds lay the smallest eggs of any bird. Some are the size of a coffee bean!

Sword-billed hummingbird

GUIANAN COCK-OF-THE-ROCK

If you want to see a show, settle down to watch a troop of cock-of-the-rocks. Groups of males and females all gather in one area and the males dance. They bob and hop, showing off their splendid orange crests and making a variety of calls. The females pick the best perfomer.

WHERE IN THE WORLD?

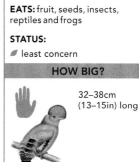

LIVES: lowland forest, northeastern South America

EATS: fruit, seeds, insects, reptiles and frogs

STATUS:
least concern

HOW BIG?

32–38cm (13–15in) long

The male is more brightly colored than the brown female.

The male's crest is made up of two layers of orange feathers, all tipped with black.

SPOTTER FACT
To find a female, males have a competition with each other. They show off their fancy feathers and footwork.

Both the male and female have a black tail.

Guianan cock-of-the-rock

IT'S WILD! A cock-of-the-rock eats seeds that pass straight through its body. New trees grow from its poop.

MANAKINS

The best time to see manakins is when the male is showing off to a female. The male leaps and snaps his wings together, making loud cracking noises. The golden-headed manakin even does a backward "moonwalk" along a branch.

A short, wide bill is good for eating fruit.

White-bearded manakin

Most manakins have a different-colored head patch from the rest of their body.

WHERE IN THE WORLD?

A short tail fans out during the mating dance.

Look for the orange legs of the white-bearded manakin.

Blue-crowned manakin

LIVES: lowland rainforest

- White-bearded manakin, northern South America
- Blue-crowned manakin, Central America and northern South America
- Golden-headed manakin, Central and northern South America and Trinidad

EATS: fruit, insects

STATUS: least concern

HOW BIG?

White-bearded manakin 10–11cm (4in) long

Blue-crowned manakin 8–9cm (3–3.5in) long

Golden-headed manakin 8–9cm (3–3.5in) long

Manakins can make buzzing sounds with their wings.

Golden-headed manakin

BROADBILLS

Broadbills are small birds but they make mighty loud whistling and croaking calls. Some of their sounds are made with their wing feathers and they snap their bills, or beaks, together, too. The calls are given as warnings or mating calls.

Look for the broad head, flattened beak and black ear patch.

Long-tailed broadbill

WHERE IN THE WORLD?

LIVES: lowland rainforest
- ◉ Green broadbill, Borneo, Sumatra and Malaysia
- ● Long-tailed broadbill, India and Southeast Asia

EATS: fruit, invertebrates

STATUS:
- Green broadbill – near threatened
- Long-tailed broadbill – least concern

HOW BIG?

Green broadbill 20cm (8in) long

Long-tailed broadbill 25cm (10in) long

When the long-tailed broadbill is flying, it shows a white patch under its wing, which is easy to spot.

Green broadbill

Broadbills use their wings to make a loud trilling sound.

DON'T MISS!

Look for a broadbill's pear-shaped nest. It is usually hanging over a stream or river.

IT'S WILD! Broadbills know when various trees are in fruit and move around the rainforest to eat the ripe fruit.

SUPERB LYREBIRD

Here is the world's largest songbird. The superb lyrebird has a sweet, tuneful voice. It sings many songs, some with a chorus. It's also a copycat and mimics the songs of other birds and noises it hears.

It takes about seven years for a male's tail feathers to grow to their full length.

When on display, the male lyrebird's feathers look like a musical instrument called a lyre.

The lyrebird's strong legs and sharp claws help it run along branches.

Superb lyrebird

SPOTTER FACT
The superb lyrebird not only mimics birdsong, it has also been known to make car alarm sounds.

Song and dance
To attract a female, the male lyrebird puts on a show. It sings and dances with its long tail waving over its head.

WHERE IN THE WORLD?

LIVES: monsoon forest, southeastern Australia and Tasmania

EATS: invertebrates, fungi

STATUS:
🍃 least concern

HOW BIG?

100cm (39in) long (including tail)

BOWERBIRDS

Keep a lookout for an arch of woven twigs and
leaves decorated with pretty feathers and flowers.
A male bowerbird gathers together materials from
nature and builds them into an arch, called a bower,
to impress a female. He decorates the bower with
bright, shiny objects and dances in front of it.

The golden bowerbird
is the smallest of the
bowerbird family.

Golden bowerbird

The satin bowerbird's
feathers are black,
but they shine blue
in the sun.

Satin bowerbird

Look for the
satin bowerbird's
blue-black eyes.

WHERE IN THE WORLD?

LIVES: lowland rainforest
- Great bowerbird, northern Australia
- Satin bowerbird, eastern Australia
- Golden bowerbird, northeastern Australia

EATS: fruit, flowers, nectar, leaves, insects

STATUS:
- least concern

HOW BIG?

Golden bowerbird
23–25cm (9–10in) long

Great bowerbird
33–38cm (13–15in) long

Satin bowerbird
27–33cm
(11–13in) long

The male shows off his pink crest to impress a female.

DON'T MISS!
Watch as the bird decorates his bower with seeds, bones, shells, flowers, pieces of glass and plastic objects.

During the dance display, the male great bowerbird holds a colored object in his beak.

McGregor's bowerbird

Great bowerbird

Tower of love
Different bowerbird families build different-shaped bowers.

Golden bowerbird

Two towers
This bowerbird has built two connecting towers out of sticks and made an arch.

SPOTTER FACT
A male bowerbird will knock over another bird's bower to steal the shiny objects for his own.

BIRDS OF PARADISE

Take your time to watch the beautiful birds of paradise showing off their amazing colorful feathers. Often, male birds have neck ruffs and extremely long feathers called streamers. You might see some birds of paradise with fancy head plumes, too.

The magnificent riflebird has shimmering blue-green feathers around its neck.

Magnificent riflebird

The male King bird of paradise swings and swishes his tail feathers to impress a female.

Birds of paradise have long, stout beaks.

Wallace's standardwing

IN DANGER

For hundreds of years, birds of paradise have been hunted for their beautiful feathers.

The male Wallace's standardwing holds his long wing feathers over its head like a parachute when dancing for a female.

King bird of paradise

Twelve-wired bird of paradise

Look for the red eyes of this bird of paradise.

The twelve-wired bird of paradise has twelve streamers that sweep out of its tail end.

WHERE IN THE WORLD?

LIVES: lowland rainforest,

● Magificent riflebird, New Guinea, northern Australia

◉ King bird of paradise, Western Parotia, New Guinea

◌ Wallace's standardwing, eastern Indonesia

◉ Twelve-wired bird of paradise, Indonesia and New Guinea

EATS: fruit and insects

STATUS:

🍃 all least concern

HOW BIG?

Magnificent riflebird 33cm (13in) long

King bird of paradise 16cm (6in) long

Western parotia 33cm (13in) long

Twelve-wired bird of paradise 33cm (13in) long

Wallace's standardwing 28cm (11in) long

The male western parotia has three silver head streamers above eatch eye.

Western parotia

To attract a female, the male western parotia balloons his feathers up like a skirt and dances like a ballerina.

DON'T MISS!

Watch as the male twelve wired bird of paradise brushes his streamers against a female's face.

RAGGIANA BIRD OF PARADISE

Don't miss this show, called a leck. It's a competition to find a mate. In a forest clearing, a group of male raggiana birds of paradise gather. They grip the branches with strong feet and dance to show off their fantastic feathers.

The female is less colorful than the male so she can camouflage when raising chicks.

WHERE IN THE WORLD?

LIVES: lowland rainforest, Papua New Guinea

EATS: fruit, insects, leaves, frogs, lizards

STATUS:
least concern

HOW BIG?

34cm (13in) long

The female chooses the finest show bird!

Female raggiana bird of paradise

The male shakes his head and holds out his wings while displaying.

Male raggiana bird of paradise

The males make loud, high-pitched calls while they dance.

The male's feathers stick straight up into the air.

A feathery display
The male birds of paradise flock together to display. They shake their long, shimmering feathers, which they fan out to look as impressive as possible.

The long display feathers are positioned on the bird's back.

SPOTTER FACT

The dance moves of this bird of paradise have been copied for a national dance in Papua New Guinea!

In the sunshine, flaming orange feathers dazzle.

REPTILES

HOW TO SPOT REPTILES

It's hard to believe a slithering snake with no legs and a turtle with a shell and four legs belong to the same animal group, but they are both reptiles. Search carefully to spot these scaly animals lurking among the leaves and branches of the trees, or next to the water's edge.

WHAT MAKES A REPTILE?

COLD-BLOODED A reptile is cold-blooded, which means it relies on its surroundings to warm up and cool down.

SCALY SKIN A reptile's skin is made up of scales, bony plates or both.

EGGS Most reptiles lay eggs. A few give birth to live young.

VERTEBRATE A reptile is a vertebrate, which means it has a backbone.

Look at the tail
Notice how a reptile's tail helps with balance. A chameleon coils its tail around a branch.

Search at dawn
Reptiles can be difficult to spot. They are often camouflaged and very often silent. The best time to see a reptile is at dawn when it basks in the early morning sunshine to warm up.

Study the eyes
Look how the chameleon's eyes stick out and sit on each side of its head. This reptile has swiveling eyes for 360-degree, or all-round, vision.

Watch and wait
A chameleon is difficult to spot because its coat can change color. Be patient.

Be alert
Reptiles can move suddenly. The chameleon shoots out its long tongue at lightning-fast speed to catch an insect.

Chameleon

A powerful body

Many snakes in the jungle are huge. They use their strong, muscular bodies to hang from trees to snatch prey.

How do reptiles hunt and hide?

Most jungle reptiles are predators, which means they hunt and eat other animals. The animals they feed on are known as prey. Reptiles have clever ways of hunting animals they want to eat and staying safe from predators that want to eat them.

REPTILE WATCH

Imagine sitting in the heart of the jungle for some reptile spotting. It is important to take great care when you study animals. Do not do anything that could destroy their homes.

A safe shell

When a common snapping turtle is in danger, it pulls its head into its shell. A predator finds the shell hard to attack.

A strong bite

The black caiman has a toothy snout and can open its mouth wide to grab and eat large animals.

RIVER TURTLES

When you spot a river turtle, just imagine its ancestors wandering the Earth 200 million years ago. Turtles lived at the same time as the dinosaurs and have changed little since. We know this because fossils – or remains – have been found. Today, many kinds of turtles make their homes in rainforest rivers, streams and pools.

SPOTTER FACT

A turtle's shell is part of its skeleton. As a baby grows, the shell grows with the skeleton.

The alligator snapping turtle has a wormlike lump on its tongue to lure fish into its mouth.

Alligator snapping turtle

The alligator snapping turtle is the largest of the river turtles.

The common snapping turtle lies in mud, with only its eyes and nostrils showing, waiting for prey.

Common snapping turtle

WHERE IN THE WORLD?

LIVES: lowland rainforest and mangrove forest

● Alligator snapping turtle, southeastern USA

◉ Common snapping turtle, Canada, USA

◉ Twist-necked turtle, northern South America

◉ Central American river turtle, Central America

EATS: fish, frogs, birds, small reptiles and water plants

STATUS:

▰ Alligator snapping turtle – vulnerable

▰ Common snapping turtle – least concern

▰ Twist-necked turtle – least concern

▰ Central American river turtle – critically endangered

HOW BIG?

Alligator snapping turtle 66–80cm (26–31in) long

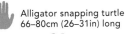

Common snapping turtle 20–36cm (8–14in) long

Twist-necked turtle 14–17cm (5.5–6.5in) long

Central American river turtle 30–65cm (12–26in) long

DON'T MISS!

Watch for a female turtle laying her round eggs on the water's edge. She lays the eggs, then leaves.

Look for the brown-and-yellow patchy shell on the twist-necked turtle.

The twist-necked turtle curls its head into its shell by twisting it to the side.

Twist-necked turtle

This turtle's thick shell is completely smooth with no ridges.

The male Central American river turtle has a golden head. The female's head is gray.

Central American river turtle

The webbed feet make it difficult for the Central American river turtle to walk on land.

BLACK CAIMAN

The black caiman is the largest predator in the rainforest. It has few enemies of its own, except jaguars and humans. Find a black caiman cooling off in the river. Look for a dark-coloured body with paler bands around the jaw. This massive alligator lurks in the water with just its eyes and ears showing above the surface.

WHERE IN THE WORLD?

LIVES: lowland rainforest, northern and central South America

EATS: fish, capybara, tapirs, deer, snakes, otters, turtles, birds and small mammals

STATUS:
🌿 least concern

HOW BIG?

3–5m (10–16ft) long

IN DANGER

The black caiman was almost hunted to extinction for its skin, which can be made into leather.

Watch for the caiman's powerful tail, which it uses to protect itself from predators.

The black caiman loves to sunbathe. Dark skin absorbs the heat of the sun and warms the reptile up.

Black caiman

The caiman's powerful jaws can shatter a turtle shell with one bite.

The caiman's black skin helps to hide it when it hunts at night.

SPOTTER FACT

If a green iguana is caught by its tail, the tail breaks off and another one grows in its place.

The green iguana has strong jaws with razor-sharp teeth.

A row of spines along the iguana's back helps to protect it from predators.

The green iguana uses its tail to whip away enemies.

Green iguana

Sharp claws are used by the iguana to climb trees.

GREEN IGUANA

A green iguana escapes a hawk or snake by falling off a high branch. Sometimes it crash-lands onto the ground, sometimes into the water. In the daytime, spot this large lizard at the tops of the trees feeding on leaves, flowers and fruit.

WHERE IN THE WORLD?

LIVES: lowland rainforest, Mexico, Central America, the Caribbean and southern Brazil

EATS: leaves, flowers and fruit

STATUS:
🔹 least concern

HOW BIG?

100–200cm (39–79in) long

GREEN BASILISK LIZARD

This bright green lizard can run on water – fast! When in danger, it drops from a tree and scampers quickly across the top of the water for a short while, then swims to freedom.

SPOTTER FACT

A female lays up to twenty eggs in a hole, then runs off. When the babies are born they look after themselves.

Folded skin between the toes unfolds to help the basilisk lizard run on water.

The long tail, held up high, helps the basilisk lizard to balance when it runs.

Green basilisk lizard

WHERE IN THE WORLD?

LIVES: lowland rainforest, Central America

EATS: insects, small mammals, small lizards, fruit and flowers

STATUS:
least concern

HOW BIG?

60–76cm (24–30in) long

IT'S WILD! The male green basilisk raises his head crest to impress females.

CHINESE WATER DRAGON

Look for a Chinese water dragon along the river's edge and in the low branches of overhanging trees. They live in groups with one male and several females.

SPOTTER FACT

A Chinese water dragon can sleep in the water with just its nostrils above the surface.

The water dragon puffs up its throat to look bigger when threatened.

The water dragon's whiplike tail is a weapon.

Chinese water dragon

Look for bands of color on the tail.

WHERE IN THE WORLD?

LIVES: lowland rainforest, China and Southeast Asia

EATS: insects, fish, small mammals, reptiles and plants

STATUS:
vulnerable

HOW BIG?

60–100cm
(24–39in) long

A water dragon's tail is two-thirds of its body length.

DON'T MISS!

Watch a Chinese water dragon stay underwater for up to ninety minutes to escape being eaten.

COMMON GREEN FOREST LIZARD

When a male is ready to mate, his head and throat turn bright red.

Keep trekking uphill into the mountain forest to see the common green forest lizard. Here's how to spot one. Look for a wide head with a hollow in the forehead and sunken cheeks. The male is more colorful than the female.

The forest lizard's long tail can curl around branches to help it balance.

WHERE IN THE WORLD?

LIVES: lowland rainforest and monsoon forest, India and Sri Lanka

EATS: insects

STATUS:
🌿 least concern

HOW BIG?

30cm (12in) long

SPOTTER FACT

Conelike spines down the lizard's back trick other animals into thinking the lizard is bigger than it really is.

Notice striped markings on the tail.

Common green forest lizard

PARSON'S CHAMELEON

A chameleon is famously difficult to spot because it changes colors depending on its mood. It waits, camouflaged in the trees, swiveling its eyes to see prey. Then it swiftly shoots out a long, sticky tongue and swallows an insect whole.

WHERE IN THE WORLD?

LIVES: lowland rainforest, Madagascar

EATS: plants, insects and small birds

STATUS:

◢ near threatened

HOW BIG?

60–70cm (24–27in) long

Parson's chameleon

The parson's chameleon has flexible toes that grip branches.

A long tail curls and grips to help the chameleon climb and balance.

IT'S WILD! Chameleons come in a rainbow of colors from bright pink to electric blue.

KUHL'S FLYING GECKO

Keen-eyed animal spotters, take note! The Kuhl's flying gecko is camouflaged to look like rough-patterned, brown tree bark. Spotting the gecko's eyes might be the only way to see it gliding between the trees.

SPOTTER FACT

Geckos make more noises than most lizards. They squeak, click, croak and hiss.

The Kuhl's flying gecko rests with its head down before it leaps off a branch.

Flaps open on either side of the gecko's body to help it glide.

WHERE IN THE WORLD?

LIVES: lowland rainforest, Asia

EATS: crickets and worms

STATUS:
 least concern

HOW BIG?

12–20cm (5–8in) long

The gecko has no eyelids. It licks its eyes clean with its tongue.

While gliding, the flying gecko spreads out its webbed feet.

Kuhl's flying gecko

EMERALD TREE MONITOR

Keep your eyes on the emerald tree monitor – if it gets spooked, it's off in a flash. Long toes with sharp claws grip onto tree bark to help the monitor run. Its light, slender body enables it to race along thin branches.

SPOTTER FACT

A female emerald tree monitor may lay her eggs in a termite mound. When the babies hatch, they eat the termites.

Look for the black stripes that run across the tree monitor's back.

The emerald tree monitor's green color hides it among the leaves.

Long toes with sharp claws help the tree monitor to grip onto branches.

An extremely long tail curls around branches to help the tree monitor balance.

Emerald tree monitor

WHERE IN THE WORLD?

LIVES: lowland rainforest and mangrove forest, New Guinea and nearby islands

EATS: insects, spiders, crabs, frogs, geckos, birds and small mammals

STATUS:
least concern

HOW BIG?

75–100cm (30–39in) long

IT'S WILD! The emerald tree monitor sleeps on a branch, gripping with its claws and holding on with its tail.

KOMODO DRAGON

Warning! A Komodo dragon is dangerous to mammals big and small. This gigantic lizard has large, gray scales on its tough body, a long tail for lashing out, short, strong legs that run fast and a powerful, venomous bite.

DON'T MISS!

Watch the Komodo dragon about to pounce on prey. It stands up high on its hind legs and tail.

The thick, leathery skin of this lizard is made up of small scales, which which fall in folds at the neck.

The Komodo dragon has a huge stomach. It can eat almost its own weight in one meal!

The Komodo dragon has about sixty sharp teeth that are replaced whenever they fall out.

SPOTTER FACT

When threatened, a Komodo dragon will throw up its food. It runs faster when lighter.

Sharp claws help the Komodo dragon to dig burrows and unearth food.

WHERE IN THE WORLD?

LIVES: lowland rainforest, Lesser Sunda Islands, Indonesia

EATS: deer, pigs, smaller Komodo dragons and water buffalo

STATUS:
vulnerable

HOW BIG?

2–3m (6.5–10ft) long

The Komodo dragon "tastes" the air with its forked tongue to hunt its prey.

Lasting bite
The Komodo dragon is one of the few lizards in the world that has a venomous bite. All it has to do is bite its prey once and wait. It takes about three or four hours for its victim to die.

The long, thick tail is used as a weapon. It is also used to balance the Komodo dragon when standing on its hind legs.

Komodo dragon

IN DANGER
In 1980, Indonesia created the Komodo National Park to protect the lizard's home.

The Komodo dragon lifts its body high off the ground, which helps it to run quickly.

GREEN ANACONDA

WHERE IN THE WORLD?

The green anaconda is massive. It eats wild pigs, deer, birds, turtles, capybaras, caimans and even jaguars. First, it squeezes the animal to death, then it opens its jaws wide and swallows the body – whole.

LIVES: lowland rainforest, South America

EATS: wild pigs, deer, capybara birds, turtles, caimans and jaguars

STATUS:
least concern

HOW BIG?

6–9m (20–30ft) long

SPOTTER FACT

A green anaconda can swallow a jaguar whole. Afterward, it won't need to eat for weeks or even months.

The green anaconda can hold its breath underwater for ten minutes.

Green anaconda

The green anaconda is the heaviest snake in the world.

The female anaconda is larger than the male.

IT'S WILD! When a baby green anaconda is born, it is as long as your arm.

The emerald tree boa lives at the tops of the trees. It waits to attack an animal on the branches below.

The emerald tree boa's tongue collects scents, or smells, to find prey.

Emerald tree boa

Look for the bold stripes that look like a carpet.

The carpet python is not venomous, but it has a painful bite.

WHERE IN THE WORLD?

LIVES: lowland rainforest

- Emerald tree boa, South America
- Carpet python, Australia, New Guinea

EATS: small mammals, lizards, birds, bats and frogs

STATUS:

least concern

HOW BIG?

Carpet python 180–240cm 71–94in) long

Emerald tree boa 180cm (71in) long

Carpet python

TREE SNAKES

On the ground, the air is warm and sticky. It's hot in the trees, too, where tree snakes thrive. Their slender bodies glide along the branches, stretching out to reach the next tree ahead.

SPOTTER FACT

Tree snakes have nose holes that can sense the heat of an animal. They use these to hunt prey at night.

IT'S WILD! Emerald tree boa babies are born orange or red. They gradually turn green over their first year.

COMMON BOA CONSTRICTOR

In the jungle, it's every animal for itself. A common boa constrictor grabs a monkey, coils itself around the animal's body and squeezes hard, until there's no life left. It's hard to believe, but the boa opens its jaws wide enough to eat the monkey whole.

Common boa constrictor

WHERE IN THE WORLD?

LIVES: lowland rainforest, South and Central America

EATS: small and medium mammals, reptiles and birds

STATUS:
🌿 least concern

HOW BIG?

2–4m (6.5–13ft) long

The diamond pattern on the boa's skin helps to provide camouflage.

Powerful muscles all the way down the boa constrictor's body squeeze its prey hard.

SPOTTER FACT
The female boa constrictor does not lay eggs. She gives birth to up to sixty live young.

Open wide!
The boa's jaws can open incredibly wide to swallow an animal whole. The teeth curve backwards to stop the prey from escaping.

IT'S WILD! After eating a monkey or a pig, the boa doesn't need to eat again for weeks!

COOK'S TREE BOA

Ambush! Watch out for a surprise attack by the Cook's tree boa. First it hangs from a branch by its tail, then in one quick move, bites and coils its body around a bird.

SPOTTER FACT

The Cook's tree boa's long, thin body, helps it to crawl along narrow branches, stretching from one to another.

The boa's tough scales are flexible to allow the snake to move its body in coils.

The Cook's tree boa moves silently to surprise its victim.

SPOTTER FACT

The Cook's tree boa is found only on one tiny island in the Caribbean.

WHERE IN THE WORLD?

LIVES: lowland rainforest, St. Vincent, Caribbean

EATS: rats, bats, squirrels, lizards and small monkeys

STATUS:
 status unknown

HOW BIG?

150cm (60in) long

Large eyes help this snake to hunt at night.

Cook's tree boa

IT'S WILD! The Cook's tree boa's bite does not contain venom, or poison, but it's still painful.

MILK SNAKE

Be aware of copycat snakes. A young milk snake is harmless but has a bright, stripy skin that looks like a venomous, or poisonous, coral snake. This helps protect the milk snake from predators.

Look for the milk snake's black bands next to the red bands.

WHERE IN THE WORLD?

LIVES: lowland rainforest
- Milk snake, Central and northern South America
- Coral snake, northern South America

EATS: insects, small lizards, mice, voles, rats, eggs and snakes

STATUS:
🌿 least concern

HOW BIG?

Milk snake 35cm–100cm (14–39in) long	Ecuadorian coral snake 60–90cm (24–35in) long

The milk snake can vibrate its tail, making a rattle, if it feels threatened.

Milk snake

SPOTTER FACT
If the milk snake is under attack, it lets out a stinky-smelling liquid from under its tail end.

Which is which?
Can you tell the difference? It takes an expert to tell which is the venomous coral snake and which is the harmless milk snake.

Ecuadorian coral snake

When the snake chews its prey, venom releases slowly and kills the animal.

The dark color camouflages it on the forest floor.

Mangrove snake

Look for the yellow bands on the snake's body, which don't join all the way round.

SPOTTER FACT

A mangrove snake is also known as the gold-ringed cat snake because its eyes look like a cat's.

MANGROVE SNAKE

WHERE IN THE WORLD?

LIVES: lowland rainforest and mangrove forest, Southeast Asia

EATS: frogs, lizards, eggs, fish and small mammals

STATUS:
least concern

HOW BIG?

150–200cm (59–79in) long

To see a mangrove snake in the day, you will need to be high up. At the top of the tallest tree, this slender, black-and-yellow snake basks in the sunshine, warming up its body. At night it slides down to the ground to hunt.

KING COBRA

A king cobra is shy. But beware, when threatened, this snake lifts the top of its body to stand tall enough to look a person in the eye. It flares up its "hood" and growls ferociously.

WHERE IN THE WORLD?

LIVES: lowland rainforest and mangrove forest, India, southern China and Southeast Asia

EATS: snakes, lizards, eggs and small mammals

STATUS: vulnerable

HOW BIG?

1.5-5.5m (5-18ft) long

DON'T MISS!

Keep a watch for two males wrestling over a female. The winner pins the other one down!

SPOTTER FACT

A king cobra can deliver enough venom, or poison, in one bite to kill an elephant.

When the king cobra rears up, it hisses loudly, almost sounding like it's growling.

The king cobra's "hood" flares to frighten off predators.

A king cobra spends most of the time on the ground, but can also climb trees and swim.

A fully grown king cobra has yellow or white wavy markings.

King cobra

IT'S WILD! The king cobra is the longest venomous snake. Lay three adult humans end to end in a row and that's how long a cobra can grow!

VIPERS

Beware of the vipers. These well-camouflaged snakes do not always dart away if disturbed. They are more likely to lunge out and bite with their long fangs, injecting their dangerous venom.

White-lipped tree viper

Look out for a viper's wide, triangular head.

The hognosed pit viper is named after its upturned nose, which is like a pig's.

The rhino viper has hornlike scales on the end of its nose.

Hognosed pit viper

Rhino viper

SPOTTER FACT

Vipers have long, hollow fangs. As they bite, the fangs unfold and inject venom.

The bushmaster is the longest viper. It is also the most venomous.

Bushmaster

The Malayan pit viper is aggressive and bites many humans each year.

Malayan pit viper

WHERE IN THE WORLD?

LIVES: lowland rainforest

- White-lipped tree viper, Southeast Asia
- Hognosed viper, Mexico, Central America, northern South America
- Rhino viper, West and Central Africa
- Bushmaster, central and northern South America
- Malayan pit viper, Southeast Asia

EATS: small mammals, frogs, fish and lizards

STATUS:
- bushmaster – vulnerable
- others – least concern

HOW BIG?

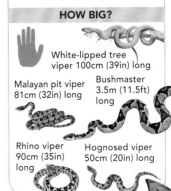

White-lipped tree viper 100cm (39in) long

Malayan pit viper 81cm (32in) long

Bushmaster 3.5m (11.5ft) long

Rhino viper 90cm (35in) long

Hognosed viper 50cm (20in) long

AMPHIBIANS

HOW TO SPOT AMPHIBIANS

A tiny tree frog leaps through the dripping leaves and a caecilian slithers through a running stream. Amphibians all have one main thing in common – they need to live near water. The damp jungle is a perfect place to spot amphibians.

WHAT MAKES AN AMPHIBIAN?

BREATHING Most adult amphibians breathe through lungs and their skin. Tadpoles breathe through gills.

COLD-BLOODED An amphibian is cold-blooded, which means it relies on its surroundings to warm up and cool down.

EGGS Most amphibians lay eggs, either on or in water. Their young live in water.

SKIN Amphibians have smooth, moist skin.

VERTEBRATE An amphibian is a vertebrate, which means it has a backbone.

Head for water
Listen for a splash. A plop of water can let you know a jumping frog or toad might be nearby. Often the best time to hear frogs is at dusk. They gather in ponds and croak to attract mates.

Look at the skin
Brightly colored skin often means an animal is poisonous. Predators know not to eat the dyeing dart frog.

Ask questions
What exactly am I looking at? This is a caecilian, which is an amphibian with no legs.

Dyeing dart frog

Ringed caecilian

Notice the feet shape
Most frogs have webbed feet – flaps of skin between the toes to help them swim. A dyeing dart frog has long fingers to grip branches instead.

Where do frogs live?

The rainforest has enough rain to allow frogs and toads to live in the damp treetops, as well as in ponds and rivers. Their strong legs help them to leap from branch to branch.

AMPHIBIAN WATCH

Imagine there is a tropical rainstorm in the rainforest. Some rainforest leaves catch water and hold it, creating little pools. You peep inside and might find a frog taking a dip.

Feet that glide

The Wallace's flying frog jumps from tree to tree. It has webbed feet that spread out to help it land softly.

Poisonous skin

The blue poison frog is bright blue. This is a warning to other animals that it is dangerous to eat.

Life cycle of a frog

A frog goes through a series of changes, called metamorphosis. A frog lays eggs. The eggs hatch into tadpoles, which grow into froglets, then frogs.

CAECILIANS

Don't be fooled! This wriggling animal, with its bullet-shaped head, might look like a snake, which is a reptile, but a caecilian is a legless amphibian. Caecilians live underground, so they are difficult to spot, but you might see one in the shallow waters of a stream.

SPOTTER FACT

Caecilians come in different sizes – from the length of your thumb to as long as you are tall!

WHERE IN THE WORLD?

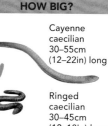

LIVES: lowland rainforest, northern South America

EATS: insect larvae, shrimps, small fish, frogs and lizards, small snakes and worms

STATUS:
least concern

HOW BIG?

Cayenne caecilian 30–55cm (12–22in) long

Ringed caecilian 30–45cm (12–18in) long

Look for the white stripes on the ringed caecilian.

Ringed caecilian

Caecilians can't see well, but they have a good sense of smell.

A fin on the tail helps the caecilian to swim fast.

Cayenne caecilian

Built for burrowing
A bony skull with powerful jaw muscles pushes caecilians through the soil.

IT'S WILD! If attacked by a predator, a caecilian can let a poisonous slime out of its skin.

SURINAM TOAD

It's difficult to spot a Surinam toad camouflaged in the river, but keep watching that mottled rock that seems to move. The most suprising thing about this frog is how baby froglets grow on their mother's back.

DON'T MISS!
The Surinam toad has no tongue and no teeth. Watch as it grabs prey in its fingers and swallows it whole!

The male pushes the eggs onto the female's back. Then a honeycomb of skin bubbles grow to keep them safe.

Surinam toad

The Surinam toad's eggs hatch into tadpoles on the mother's back. They remain there while they turn into froglets.

Tiny, lidless eyes sit on top of the Surinam toad's head.

WHERE IN THE WORLD?

LIVES: lowland rainforest, northern South America, Trinidad and Tobago

EATS: insects, small fish, crustaceans and worms

STATUS:
least concern

HOW BIG?

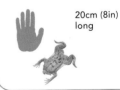

20cm (8in) long

A flat body camouflages the toad on the swamp floor and riverbed.

Waiting in ambush
At the end of each front foot, star-shaped toes sense any animal movement nearby. The Surinam toad waits, then gulps down an insect.

TREE FROGS

A small tree frog jumps through its canopy home, where the rain is falling and dangling vines drip with water. The frog jumps from a large, shiny leaf and lands on a slippery branch. At liftoff, the frog's long legs spring. On landing, its sticky toes grip.

The red-eyed tree frog's huge, bulging eyes help the frogs to judge distances well.

The red-eyed tree frog closes its eyes and hides its hands to camouflage itself.

Red-eyed tree frog

WHERE IN THE WORLD?

LIVES: lowland rainforest
- ◉ wLa Loma tree frog, Central America
- ● Red-eyed tree frog, Mexico, Central America, and northern South America
- ◉ Rusty tree frog, Central and northern South America
- ◎ Veined tree frog, Central and northern South America, Trinidad and Tobago
- ◉ White's tree frog, Australia and New Guinea

EATS: insects, spiders and worms

STATUS:
- ◤ La Loma tree frog – critically endangered
- ◢ other tree frogs – least concern

HOW BIG?

Red-eyed tree frog
5–7cm (2–2.8in) long

La Loma tree frog
3cm (1in) long

Veined tree frog
6.4–11cm (2.5–4.3in) long

Rusty tree frog
10–12cm (4–4.7in) long

White's tree frog
7–12cm (2.8–4.7in) long

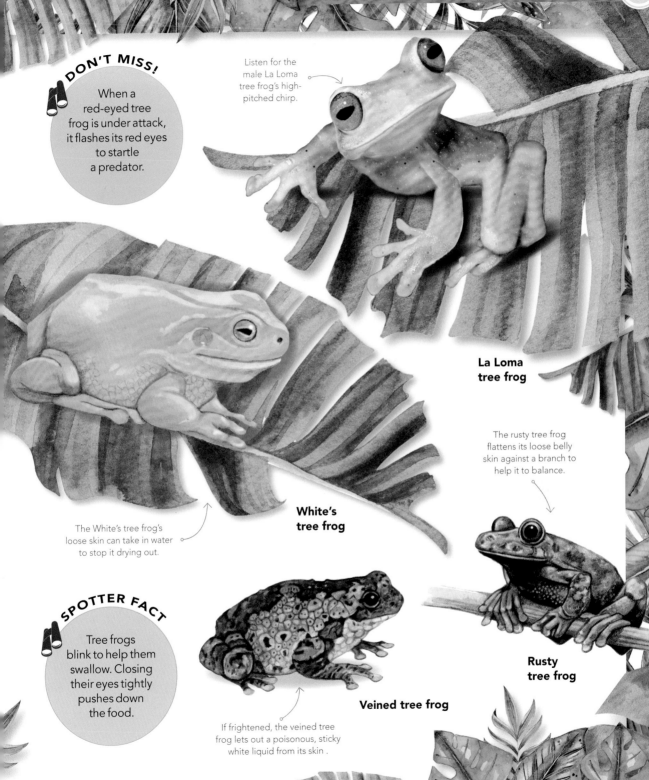

DON'T MISS!

When a red-eyed tree frog is under attack, it flashes its red eyes to startle a predator.

Listen for the male La Loma tree frog's high-pitched chirp.

La Loma tree frog

The rusty tree frog flattens its loose belly skin against a branch to help it to balance.

The White's tree frog's loose skin can take in water to stop it drying out.

White's tree frog

SPOTTER FACT

Tree frogs blink to help them swallow. Closing their eyes tightly pushes down the food.

Veined tree frog

If frightened, the veined tree frog lets out a poisonous, sticky white liquid from its skin .

Rusty tree frog

GOLIATH FROG

WHERE IN THE WORLD?

LIVES: lowland rainforest, western Africa

EATS: spiders, worms, insects, crabs, baby turtles and small snakes

STATUS:
◢ endangered

HOW BIG?

80cm (31in) long (including the legs)

Look into a jungle waterfall to spot the enormous goliath frog. It is the biggest frog in the world – as big as a pet cat. But you won't hear a goliath frog, because it can't croak.

Powerful legs help the goliath frog to push heavy rocks to make a pond for its nest.

The goliath frog catches insects with its long, sticky tongue.

Long toes stretch out to be fully webbed to help the frog swim.

Goliath frog

COQUI

SPOTTER FACT

Usually, a female's eggs hatch into tadpoles, but a coqui's eggs hatch into tiny froglets.

At dusk, listen for the male coqui's loud, high-pitched "ko-kEE" call. The males compete to attract females using sounds.

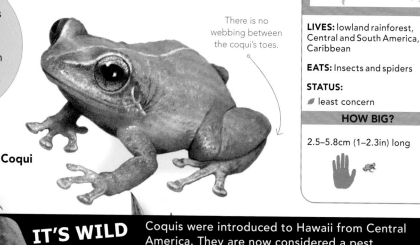

There is no webbing between the coqui's toes.

Coqui

WHERE IN THE WORLD?

LIVES: lowland rainforest, Central and South America, Caribbean

EATS: Insects and spiders

STATUS:
◢ least concern

HOW BIG?

2.5–5.8cm (1–2.3in) long

IT'S WILD Coquis were introduced to Hawaii from Central America. They are now considered a pest.

Glass frogs are excellent tree climbers.

GLASS FROGS

It's really difficult to spot a glass frog because its underneath is see-through, just like glass. Sometimes, if you see a glass frog from below, you can see its heart pumping blood around the body. Glass frogs are well camouflaged and stay almost completely hidden.

Glass frog

Listen for the three-note "chee-chee-chee" of the Nicaragua glass frog.

Look for the dark spots on the Nicaragua glass frog's back.

Nicaragua glass frog

WHERE IN THE WORLD?

LIVES: lowland rainforest, Central America and northern South America

EATS: insects, spiders, other frogs

STATUS:
🌿 endangered

HOW BIG?

Glass frog 2–3.2cm (0.8–1.3in) long

Nicaragua glass frog 3cm (1in) long

DON'T MISS!

Watch a male glass frog guard a clutch of eggs. He keeps the eggs wet.

Sticky eggs

A female lays eggs underneath a leaf above water. The eggs stick to the leaf. When the tadpoles hatch, they drop into the water.

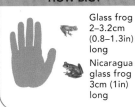

POISON ARROW FROGS

In the jungle, poison arrow frogs thrive in the rain and heat. Some kinds live in the canopy, others on the forest floor. Many are tiny, about the size of your thumbnail. Most have poison in their skin. Their bright colours warn predators to "keep away!"

Poison arrow frogs have suction pads on their toes to help them grip onto branches.

Listen for the granular poison frog. It is noisy, croaking for hours without stopping.

Blue poison frog

Granular poison frog

The poison on the frog's skin comes from the food it eats.

Harlequin poison dart frog

WHERE IN THE WORLD?

LIVES: lowland rainforest, Central and South America

LIVES: insects, spiders, mites and centipedes

STATUS:
- Dyeing dart frog – least concern
- Harlequin poison dart frog – critically endangered
- Strawberry poison frog – least concern
- Blue poison frog – endangered
- Granular poison frog – vulnerable
- Golden poison frog – endangered

HOW BIG?

Dyeing dart frog 5cm (2in) long

Harlequin poison dart frog 4cm (1.5in) long

Strawberry poison frog 1.7–2.4cm (0.7–0.9in) long

Blue poison frog 2.5–3.8cm (1–1.5in) long

Granular poison frog 2cm (0.8in) long

Golden poison frog 2.5cm (1in) long

The poison of one golden poison frog could kill ten people!

A strawberry poison frog carries its tadpole on its back to take it to a pool of water.

Golden poison frog

Strawberry poison frog

SPOTTER FACT

Some people who live in the Amazon rainforest dip their arrows in a frog's poison for hunting.

Tadpole pool
Some plants are shaped like cups and hold rainwater. Many poison arrow frogs drop their tadpoles into these leaf ponds after they hatch.

Bromeleid plant

It is thought that poison arrow frogs lay extra eggs for their tadpoles to eat.

Dyeing dart frog

WALLACE'S FLYING FROG

Look for patches of blue sky at the tops of the trees. You might also see a Wallace's flying frog falling gently – almost parachuting – between the branches. Notice the large webbed feet that help to control its fall.

The frog's large eyes see well to judge exactly where to land.

Flaps on the sides of the body of the frog also fan out to help it glide.

SPOTTER FACT

A female lays her eggs in a bubbly liquid on a plant above water. When they hatch, the tadpoles fall in.

Wallace's flying frog

Large toe pads help the frog land softly. They stick to the ridges of a tree trunk.

Wallace's flying frogs can jump and swim well.

High flyer
This frog spends all its time gliding through the trees. It travels to the ground only to lay eggs near water.

WHERE IN THE WORLD?

LIVES: lowland rainforest, Southeast Asia

EATS: insects

STATUS:
least concern

HOW BIG?

10cm (4in) long

HAIRY FROG

This frog is an extraordinary specimen. To stay safe from an attacker, it can break the bones in its toe pads so they burst through the skin, almost like claws. Also, hairy frog tadpoles have teeth and eat insects.

SPOTTER FACT

This frog is also known as the Wolverine frog because of the claws it can shoot out of its feet.

The claws in the hairy frog's feet make its fingers look knobbly.

Unusually for a frog, the hairy frog has several rows of teeth.

The hairs help the hairy frog to breathe underwater because it has only small lungs, which take in oxygen.

WHERE IN THE WORLD?

LIVES: lowland rainforest, Central Africa

EATS: centipedes, spiders and insects

STATUS:
🍃 least concern

HOW BIG?

11cm (4.5in) long

IT'S WILD! In the breeding season, the male hairy frog grows hairs so he can stay underwater to guard the eggs. The hairs help him to breathe.

FISH

HOW TO SPOT FISH

A hatchetfish seems to fly through the air, an electric eel looks like a swimming snake and an arapaima makes a gulping cough noise. These animals all belong to the animal group called fish.

WHAT MAKES A FISH?

GILLS A fish lives underwater and breathes using gills.

COLD-BLOODED A fish is cold-blooded, which means it relies on its surroundings to warm up and cool down.

SCALES Most fish have scales all over their bodies.

VERTEBRATE A fish is a vertebrate, which means it has a backbone.

Sit by a river
Look for tiny ripples at the water's edge, especially near rocks and gnarly tree roots. You are likely to spot a shoal of jungle fish.

Study the scales
Learn to recognize a fish by its coloring and pattern. The hatchetfish has a brown, marbled pattern.

Notice small movements
When feeding, a hatchetfish leaps out of the water to catch insects.

Marbled hatchetfish

Look, then look again
From above, these tiny hatchetfish can look like fallen leaves.

A tail to lunge
The arapaima has fins near the back of its body and a powerful tail, which helps it to lunge at great speeds toward prey.

How do fish move?
A fish moves its tail from side to side to swim through the water. Fins on the sides of its body help it to steer. Fish have specially shaped fins and tails to help them move in different ways.

Fins to hide
The angelfish's long fins and tail streamers look like reeds in the water for camouflage.

FISH WATCH

Imagine sitting by the river in the rainforest. Now look up at the sky. To spot fish, you need to keep your eyes on the birds! River birds dive headfirst into the water to catch fish.

Swimming on the bottom
An electric eel has a long fin under its body to swim through the river plants along the riverbed.

SPLASH TETRA

The female splash tetra fish leaps right out of the river to lay her eggs on overhanging leaves. Once the eggs are laid, the male keeps the eggs damp by splashing them from below until they hatch.

SPOTTER FACT

The male tetra keeps the eggs on the leaf damp by splashing them every few minutes.

WHERE IN THE WORLD?

LIVES: lowland rainforest, northern South America

EATS: worms, crustaceans and insects that fall into the water

STATUS: status unknown

HOW BIG?

5–8cm (2–3in) long

The splash tetra uses its strong tail to jump out of the water.

The splash tetra has a dark line between the mouth and the eye.

Splash tetra

DON'T MISS!

The male and female tetra make hundreds of eggs on a leaf. They keep leaping and lay six eggs at a time.

The fins on the splash tetra are far back on its body to help it grip onto leaves.

Leaf leap
To lay eggs, both fish grip onto a leaf for about ten seconds. The female lays the eggs and the male fertilizes them. After a few days the eggs hatch and the babies fall into the water below.

IT'S WILD! A tetra fish is difficult to keep as a pet because it leaps out of an aquarium.

MARBLED HATCHETFISH

The hatchetfish is named after the shape of its belly, which looks like a small, square ax called a hatchet. This little fish jumps high out of the water to catch flying insects and to avoid predators.

WHERE IN THE WORLD?

LIVES: lowland rainforest, South America

EATS: plants and insects

STATUS:
🌿 least concern

HOW BIG?

3–4cm (1–1.5in) long

SPOTTER FACT

When alarmed, the hatchetfish floats on its side at the surface, disguising itself as a leaf!

Large fins on the marbled hatchetfish help it jump out of the water.

Look out for the marble patterns on the marbled hatchetfish.

Marbled hatchetfish

The line down the body of the hatchetfish looks like the vein of a leaf and shines gold in sunlight.

ELECTRIC EEL

In the wet season, heavy rains flood the river and electric eels swim deep into the jungle along the new streams. In the dry season, there's less rain and the eels live in pools near the river's edge.

The electric eel has no scales. Its skin is completely smooth.

When the electric eel sends out a shock, its whole body becomes electric.

Electric eel

The electric eel also uses its electricty to find its way through muddy water.

WHERE IN THE WORLD?

LIVES: lowland rainforest, South America

EATS: fish, insects, crustaceans

STATUS:
least concern

HOW BIG?

2–2.5m (6.5–8ft) long

DON'T MISS!

Watch for an eel at the surface. Folds of skin at its mouth absorb air and help it breathe underwater.

IT'S WILD! The electric eel produces enough electricity in one moment to light seven light bulbs.

PIRANHAS

Don't trail your fingers in the water over the edge of the boat. A piranha has teeth as sharp as blades. It might think you are food and bite. There are many kinds of piranha. Some are more fierce than others.

HOW BIG?

Black piranha 40–45cm (16–18in) long

Red-bellied piranha 30–33cm (12–13in) long

A powerful tail helps the piranha to swim at super-fast speeds.

The piranha has an incredibly strong bite.

Black piranha

The black piranha is the largest of the the piranhas.

Usually a red-bellied piranha attacks head or tail first. This stops the prey in its tracks.

DON'T MISS!

Listen for shoals of hundreds of red-bellied piranhas. They make sounds like short barks.

At dusk, look out for red-bellied piranha when they go hunting.

Red-bellied piranha

FRESHWATER ANGELFISH

Freshwater angelfish take great care of their young. A female lays her eggs on a leaf in the water, then she and the male fan the eggs with their fins for three days. Freshwater angelfish live in pairs. They mate and look after their young and hunt for food together.

WHERE IN THE WORLD?

LIVES: lowland rainforest, northern South America

EATS: small fish and other water animals

STATUS:

 status unknown

HOW BIG?

12–15cm (5–6in) long

The freshwater angelfish is silvery in color. Look for the dark stripes down its body.

Long, reedlike fins help to hide the angelfish among the river plants.

Angelfish are slow swimmers because of their long tail and fins.

Freshwater angelfish

SPOTTER FACT

A male and a female angelfish are partners for life, and don't find another mate if one dies.

ARAPAIMA

Keep your eyes scanning the surface of the swampy river. You might spot the arapaima coming up for air. Every fifteen minutes it pops out of the water to breathe through its mouth. Listen for the gulping sound it makes, almost like a cough.

DON'T MISS!

An arapaima sometimes leaps high out of the water to grab a monkey or a bird.

Arapaima

Look for the flashes of red on the fins and tail when the fish arrives at the surface.

The arapaima's fins are near the tail to help it make powerful lunges at its prey.

When a male needs to protect his babies, he holds them in his mouth.

WHERE IN THE WORLD?

LIVES: lowland rainforest, northern South America

EATS: fish, lizards, birds, small mammals, insects, fruit and seeds

STATUS:
◣ status unknown

HOW BIG?

2–3m
(6.5–10ft) long

INVERTEBRATES

HOW TO SPOT INVERTEBRATES

A spider swings from its web, a stick insect crawls along a log and a butterfly flutters high among the leaves in the canopy. These animals may move in different ways but they are all invertebrates. Millions of mini-beasts lurk in the understory—the tangle of low branches and shrubs near the ground.

WHAT MAKES AN INVERTEBRATE?

NO SKELETON An invertebrate does not have a skeleton inside its body.

EXOSKELETON Some invertebrates have a tough outer shell called an exoskeleton.

EGGS Most invertebrates hatch from eggs.

METAMORPHOSIS Many invertebrates go through a series of changes as they grow, called metamorphosis.

COLD-BLOODED An invertebrate is cold-blooded, which means it relies on its surroundings to warm up and cool down.

Has it got an exoskeleton?
Like many invertebrates, the tarantula has a hard body case called an exoskeleton. This keeps it safe from attack and stops it drying out.

Look low
As you walk, look for invertebrates on the ground, especially near the roots of the trees. But you will need to look hard, because these animals spend their time hiding to keep safe.

Key features
To help identify a particular invertebrate, keep an eye out for its most obvious feature. All spiders have hairs on their legs.

Count the legs
Many invertebrates have six legs, but spiders like this Thailand black tarantula have eight.

When to go bug spotting
Find out which invertebrates come out when. This tarantula climbs out of its burrow at night and waits for prey to walk past.

Thailand black tarantula

How do invertebrates live?

Invertebrates that live in the jungle are food for many other animals. These invertebrates have clever ways to keep safe from predators and find their own prey to eat.

INVERTEBRATE WATCH

Imagine zooming in with binoculars to study a spider spinning its web. Watch as it waits for an insect to fly into its trap. When the spider feels the web move, it kills the insect and wraps it in silk.

Hunting for food

The golden orb weaver's web is huge compared with its size. The big web increases the chance of catching food to eat.

Dangerous or not?

The owl butterfly's wing spots look like the eyes of a bigger creature. Looking dangerous can be a way to stay safe.

Faking it

A spiny devil walking stick looks like tree bark. If it sits still on a tree branch, other animals will not see or eat it.

SPIDERS

Look up to see spiders dangling from webs and look down to see them scuttling along the forest floor. Spiders have ingenious ways of catching their food, including setting traps and waiting in ambush. Nearly all spiders kill the animals they eat with poison.

All spiders have eight legs. Hairs on their legs help to sense danger.

If threatened, this tarantula raises its front legs to show off its venomous fangs and warn predators to keep away.

Thailand black tarantula

Silk is made inside the spider's abdomen. The spider pulls the silk out with its feet.

SPOTTER FACT

All spiders spin silk. They use it to make webs and rope swings, to wrap their eggs and to line their nests.

WHERE IN THE WORLD?

LIVES: lowland rainforest

- Brazilian wandering spider, northern South America Central America
- Huntsman spider and golden orb weaver, Australia, Africa, Asia, Americas
- Funnel-web spider, Australia
- Thailand black tarantula, Myanmar, Thailand and Cambodia

EATS: insects and other tiny creatures. The bigger spiders may eat small mammals and reptiles, birds, bats and frogs

STATUS:

- Golden orb weaver – least concern
- all the other spiders – status unknown

HOW BIG?

Measurements include legspan

Brazilian wandering spider 15cm (6in) long

Huntsman spider 30cm (12in) long

Golden orb weaver 10–12cm (4–4.5in) long

Funnel-web spider 12.5cm (5in) long

Thailand black tarantula 7.6–16cm (3–6in) long

The huntsman spider is super fast at chasing its prey.

Look for the stripes down the wandering spider's body.

Huntsman spider

Golden orb weaver

Brazilian wandering spider

An orb weaver spider spins a web more than one meter in diameter, that's about the length of your outstretched arms—tip to tip.

Long, slender legs help the golden orb weaver to spin webs.

When ready to attack, the funnel-web spider raises its front legs to show its fangs.

The Brazilian wandering spider's bite is one of the most venomous on Earth.

SPOTTER FACT

A spider squirts stomach juices onto an animal to turn it into liquid, then sucks up what's left.

The spider's fangs are filled with poison that is injected into prey.

Funnel-web spider

MANTIDS

When animal spotting, be patient. An animal spend its life hiding to keep safe. Not only can different mantids look like flowers, grass and twigs but they can also sit perfectly still. Then, quick as a flash, a mantid shoots out its front legs and snatches an animal to eat.

A mantid can turn its head to see nearly all the way round

A row of sharp spines on the mantid's front legs help it to grip prey.

Common praying mantis

A mantid folds its wings against its body until needed.

The orchid mantis looks just like an orchid flower.

Orchid mantis

An insect thinks the orchid mantis is a flower and lands, then gets eaten.

WHERE IN THE WORLD?

LIVES: lowland rainforest

- Common praying mantis, Central America, South America, Africa, Asia, Australia
- Orchid mantis, Southeast Asia

EATS: insects, spiders, small frogs, birds and lizards

STATUS:
⬩ least concern

HOW BIG?

Common praying mantis 1.3–15cm (0.5–6in) long

Orchid mantis 2.5–7.6cm (1–3in) long

SPOTTER FACT

A praying mantis is named after the way it holds its front legs – it looks as if it is praying.

IT'S WILD! The giant mantid would only just fit on an adult's hand! It eats small birds and reptiles.

SPINY DEVIL WALKING STICK

Head out at night to see the giant spiny devil walking stick insect. During the day, it hides under bark and in tree hollows. At night the stick insect goes out in search of leaves to eat in the dark understory. This insect is very well hidden. It looks just like the tree bark it likes to sit on.

DON'T MISS!

Listen for the sound of stick insect eggs falling like rain. Some females drop their eggs from a great height!

The stick insect's tough skeleton is on the outside of its body to protect it.

Sharp spines on the stick insect's back legs are used as weapons for fighting.

WHERE IN THE WORLD?

LIVES: lowland rainforest, Papua New Guinea and islands nearby

EATS: leaves

STATUS:
◢ status unknown

HOW BIG?

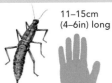

11–15cm (4–6in) long

Spiny devil walking stick

If a predator grabs the stick insect's leg, the stick insect lets it break off! It then grows a new one.

WHERE IN THE WORLD?

LIVES: lowland rainforest

- ◉ Leafcutter ant, Central and South America
- ● Army ant, Central and South America, Africa, Southeast Asia
- ◉ Bulldog ant, Australia
- ○ Weaver ant, Southeast Asia, Australia

EATS: leaves, nectar, insects, pollen

STATUS:

🍃 status unknown

HOW BIG?

Leafcutter ant 1–2cm (0.4–0.8in) long

Bulldog ant 1–4cm (0.4–1.6in) long

Army ant 0.5–1cm (0.2–0.4in) long

Weaver ant 1cm (0.4in) long

ANTS

Follow an ant and you will probably end up at an ants' nest, called a colony. Here, there might be thousands or even millions of ants, all working together to make a community. Each ant has a job to do, from gathering food to taking care of the young.

The leafcutter ant uses its jaws to cut leaves.

Leafcutter ant

An army ant worker is blind. It uses its feelers to find its way.

Army ant

DON'T MISS!

One colony of army ants can kill 100,000 creatures in one day!

The ants travel in long lines back to their nest, carrying the leaf pieces.

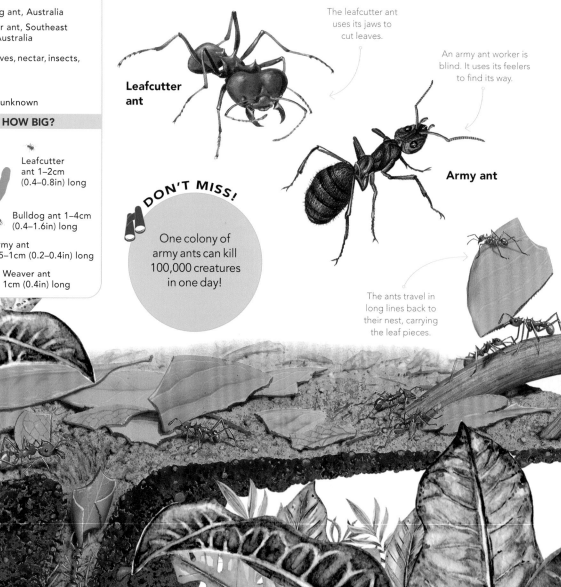

Bulldog ant

A fierce bulldog ant uses its strong jaws to bite. At the same time, it uses its venomous sting to poison.

Weaver ant

Weaver ants use silk made by their larvae to "sew" leaves together to make a nest.

Fungus farming

Leafcutter ants work together to collect and move slices of leaves to their nest. The ants don't eat the leaves. They use them to grow a fungus, which they eat.

A group of leafcutter ants can strip a tree of leaves in one day.

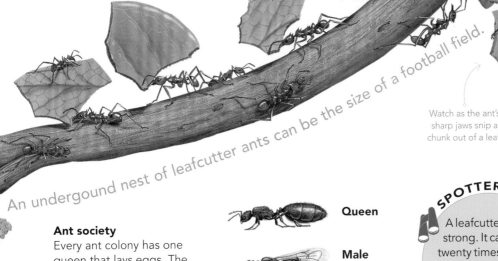

Watch as the ant's sharp jaws snip a chunk out of a leaf.

An undergound nest of leafcutter ants can be the size of a football field.

Ant society

Every ant colony has one queen that lays eggs. The males mate with the queen. Soldiers keep the colony safe. Many workers gather food.

Queen

Male

Soldier

Worker

SPOTTER FACT

A leafcutter ant is strong. It can carry twenty times its own weight. That's like you lifting two adult gorillas!

BEETLES

You won't have to look hard to see a beetle in the rainforest – there are millions! A fallen log is just the place to search, especially in the cracks and crevices. An adult beetle has two pairs of wings. The first pair acts as a hard protective suit of armor for the set of fragile wings underneath.

The goliath beetle is the largest beetle in the world. It can lift 850 times its own weight.

The front legs of the harlequin beetle are longer than its body.

Harlequin beetle

Notice the beautifully patterned wings on the harlequin beetle.

The male giraffe weevil uses his super-long neck to fight other giraffe weevils.

Giraffe weevil

Goliath beetle

Sharp claws on the goliath beetle's legs help it to grip while climbing trees.

SPOTTER FACT

Beetles help to recycle by eating dead plants and animals. This is important in the life cycle of the jungle.

WHERE IN THE WORLD?

LIVES: lowland rainforest
- Goliath beetle, Africa
- Harlequin beetle, Central America and South America
- Giraffe weevil, Madagascar
- Firefly, Asia, Central America and South
- Hercules beetle, Central America and South America

EATS: tree sap, fruit, wood. Larva may eat other insects and snails

STATUS:
🖋 status unknown

HOW BIG?

Firefly 2.5cm (1in) long

Giraffe weevil 2.5cm (1in) long

Harlequin beetle 7.5cm (3 in) long

Hercules beetle 17cm (7in) long

Goliath beetle 11cm (4in) long

Firefly

A firefly has a light at the end of its body that glows at night. Fireflies talk to each other using these lights.

DON'T MISS!
You won't miss a Hercules beetle in the air. It is one of the largest flying insects in the world.

The two parts of the horn work like pincers. A male picks up and throws down another male. The winner impresses a female.

When the beetle flies, it opens its wing cases wide and holds them open to let the wings flap.

Hercules beetle

BUTTERFLIES AND MOTHS

WHERE IN THE WORLD?

LIVES: lowland rainforest

- Owl butterfly, Central and South America
- Blue morpho, Central and South America
- Indian moon moth, Asia and Southeast Asia
- Madagascan sunset moth, Madagascar

EATS: nectar, fruit. Caterpillars eat leaves

STATUS:

🍃 status unknown

HOW BIG?

Owl butterfly 6–18cm (2.5–7in) long

Blue morpho 7.5–20 cm (3–8in) long

Indian moon moth 13–16cm (5–6in) long

Madagascan sunset moth 7–9cm (3–3.5in) long

Here are some spotting tips to help tell the difference between a butterfly and a moth. Most butterflies are brightly colored and fly in the daytime. Usually, moths are camouflaged and fly at night. A butterfly rests with its wings together, while a moth spreads its wings out wide at rest. Watch out, a few moths, including the Madagascan sunset moth, look like butterflies.

The blue morpho is easy to spot in flight. It is one of the biggest butterflies in the world!

Blue morpho

The underside of the wings are mottled brown and look just like trees. This helps to keep the morpho camouflaged from animals below.

SPOTTER FACT

When the blue morpho flies above the canopy, a pilot can see flashes of blue below the plane.

Owl-like eye spots on the owl butterfly's wings frighten predators away.

The owl butterfly flies only a short distance each time.

Owl butterfly

1. The female moon moth lays eggs on a leaf.

4. A caterpillar wraps itself into a case, called a pupa. Inside it goes through a big change.

5. A moth emerges. It stretches out its wings to dry.

3. The caterpillar grows and molts, or loses its skin, a few times.

2. The eggs turn into caterpillars, which eat a lot of leaves.

Moth life cycle

A moon moth, like all other moths and butterflies, goes through a lifecycle called metamorphosis. Each stage looks different.

The Indian moon moth has feathery antennae.

Unusually, this sunset moth is brightly colored and looks more like a butterfly.

Look for the moon moth's floating tail streamers.

Indian moon moth

SPOTTER FACT

The Indian moon moth lives as an adult for less than a week. It never eats.

Many moths come out only at night, but the sunset moth flies in the day.

Madagascan sunset moth

GIANT ATLAS MOTH

As the sun sets, watch a giant Atlas moth prepare to set off to find a mate. In the rainforest, it's hot enough to warm the flight muscles of this huge moth. It takes effort for the moth to flap its massive wings, so it flies slowly and unsteadily.

WHERE IN THE WORLD?

LIVES: lowland rainforest, Asia

EATS: the caterpillar eats leaves, as an adult it eats nothing

STATUS:
🌿 status unknown

HOW BIG?

30 cm (12in) long wingspan

The wingtips of the Atlas moth look like snake heads. This frightens off predators.

The male Atlas moth can smell a female using his feathery antennae.

Giant Atlas moth

An adult moth does not grow. All the growing is done at the caterpillar stage.

The wings are light to help the giant moth fly.

DON'T MISS!

Keep watch for a giant Atlas moth caterpillar. It's as long as an adult persons hand.

PEANUT-HEADED LANTERNFLY

The peanut-headed lanternfly is named after its bumpy, peanut-shaped head.

Peanut-headed lanternfly

The peanut-headed lanternfly acts big. When it opens its back wings, large spots look like the eyes of a much bigger animal, such as a ferocious lizard or snake.

WHERE IN THE WORLD?

LIVES: lowland rainforest, Central and South America

EATS: tree sap

STATUS:
 status unknown

HOW BIG?

9cm (3.5in) long

The peanut-headed lanternfly sucks up food from plants using mouthparts that act like a straw.

When attacked, the peanut-headed lanternfly releases a stinky spray.

SPOTTER FACT

The lanternfly knocks its head against trees to make vibrations to attract mates.

INDEX

A

agoutis 65
   Brazilian agouti 65
   gray agouti 65
   red agouti 65
Amazon 33
   river 55
amphibians 134–47
animals
   and talking 32, 39, 40, 45, 52,
      58, 59, 169
ants 8, 166–67
   army ant 166
   bulldog ant 167
   leafcutter ant 166–67
   nest 19, 93, 166
   queen 167
   soldier 167
   weaver ant 167
   worker 167
apes 36–42
   great apes 36
aye-aye 27

B

bats 22–23
   common vampire bat 22
   Honduran white bat 23
beak 11, 74, 75, 83, 87, 90, 102
bears 43–44
   sloth bear 44
   sun bear 43
beetles 168–69
   firefly 169
   giraffe weevil 168
   goliath beetle 168
   harlequin beetle 168
   Hercules beetle 169

big cats 46–48
birds 72–109
birds of paradise 106–9
   King bird of paradise 106
   magnificent riflebird 106
   raggiana bird of paradise
      108–9
   twelve wired bird of
      paradise 107
   Wallace's standardwing
      106
   western parotia 107
black caiman 113, 116, 126
bonobo 42
bowerbirds 104–5
   golden bowerbird 104
   great bowerbird 105
   McGregor's bowerbird 105
   satin bowerbird 104
broadbills 102
   green broadbill 102
   long-tailed broadbill 102
bushbaby see Demidoff
   galago
butterflies 160–61, 170
   blue morpho 10, 170
   owl butterfly 161, 170

C

caecilians 136, 138
   Cayenne caecilian 138
   ringed caecilian 136, 138
camouflage 15, 31, 38, 48,
   50, 56, 57, 71, 75, 77, 85,
   108, 121, 122, 131, 170
canopy 75
capybara 62, 126

casque 76, 97
cassowary 76
   plum 76
cats 46–51
   fishing cat 51
   ocelot 50
   swimming 50, 51
chameleon 112
   Parson's chameleon 121
chevrotains 59
   greater Malay chevrotain 59
   lesser Malay chevrotain 59
   water chevrotain 59
chimpanzee 40–41
cold-blooded 112
colugos 24, see also lemurs
   Malayan flying lemur 24
   Philippine flying lemur 24
common spotted cuscus 68
conservation 9, 11, 16, 49,
   53, 58, 85, 89, 92

D

defense 19, 44, 63, 66, 67,
   83, 91, 93, 117, 119, 165,
   170
Demidoff galago 28

E

eagles 80–81
   Congo serpent
      eagle 80
   Philippine eagle 81

echidnas 67
   long-nosed echidna 67
   short-nosed echidna 67
electric eel 151, 154
elephants 52–53
   African forest elephant 53
   Asian elephant 52
endangered animals 9, 16,
   37, 38, 41, 46, 58, 89
Equator 10
evolution 59, 114
exoskeleton 160
extinction 58, 85

F

farming 38, 41, 43, 77
fish 148–57
   freshwater angelfish 151,
      156
   arapaima 151, 157
   black piranha 155
   marbled hatchetfish
      150, 153
   red-bellied piranha 155
   splash tetra 152
      breeding 152

frogs 139–47
  blue poison frog 137, 144
  coqui 142
  dyeing dart frog 136, 145
  glass frog 143
  golden poison frog 10, 145
  goliath frog 142
  granular poison frog 144
  hairy frog 147
  Harlequin poison dart frog
    9, 144
  La Loma tree frog 141
  Nicaragua glass frog 143
  red-eyed tree frog 140
  rusty tree frog 141
  strawberry poison frog 145
  Surinam toad 139
  veined tree frog 141
  Wallace's flying frog 137, 146
  White's tree frog 141
froglets 137, 139, 142

G
giant anteater 19
  anteater young 19
giant armadillo 18
giant ground pangolin 18
gibbons 36–37
  black crested gibbon 36
  lar gibbon 36
  siamang 37
gills 150
gorilla (western lowland) 39
great apes 36
great blue turaco 95

great curassow 77
great hornbill 74, 97
Guianan cock-of-the-rock
  100

H
habitat 9
  loss 9, 33, 38, 41, 43, 75
hippopotamus (pygmy) 61
hoatzin 82
hummingbirds 8, 9, 75,
  98–99
  bee hummingbird 9,
    98–99
  collared inca 99
  crimson topaz 98
  green-throated carib 98
  purple-throated carib 98
  sword-billed hummingbird
    99
hunting 27, 31, 42, 45, 48,
  51, 131, 155
  of animals by humans 49,
    53, 58, 106, 116

I
iguana (green) 117
indri 8, 9, 26
invertebrates 158–73

J
jacamars 93
  paradise jacamar 93
  rufous-tailed jacamar 93
jaguar 15, 47, 56, 62, 126
jungle 9–11
  destruction of see habitat
    loss
  lowland rainforest 10

mangrove rainforest 10
monsoon rainforest 10

K
kangaroos 70–71
  Bennett's tree kangaroo 71
  Goodfellow's tree
    kangaroo 70

L
lemurs 24–27
  ring-tailed lemur 14, 25
leopard 48
  clouded leopard 49
lizards 117–25
  Chinese water dragon
    119
  common green forest
    lizard 120
  emerald tree monitor 123
  green basilisk lizard 118
  Komodo dragon 124–25
  Kuhl's flying gecko 11,
    122
lowland paca 64
lowland rainforest 10

M
macaws 88
  blue-and-yellow macaw 88
  hyacinth macaw 88
  scarlet macaw 88
mammals 12–71
  birth 14
  habitat 15
manakins 101
  blue-crowned manakin 101

golden-headed manakin
  101
white-bearded manakin
  101
mangrove rainforest 10
manatees 15, 54–55
  Amazonian manatee 55
  West Indian manatee 54
mantids 164
  common praying
    mantis 9, 164
  orchid mantis 164
marsupials 68–71
mating 84, 91, 101, 108
metamorphosis 160
monkeys 15, 30–35, 81, 128,
  157
  black spider monkey 15, 33
  cotton-top tamarin 30
  mandrill 35
  owl monkey 31
  proboscis monkey 34
  red howler monkey 32
monsoon rainforest 10
moths 171–72
  giant Atlas moth 172
  Indian moon moth 171
  life cycle 171
  Madagascan sunset moth
    171

N
nectar 98

O
orangutan 9, 38

P

parrots 74–75, 86–92
  blue-crowned hanging
    parrot 86
  blue-fronted parrot 87
  buff-faced pygmy
    parrot 87
  eclectus parrots 87
  kakapo 74–75, 89
  Pesquet's parrot 90
  red-fan parrot 91
  salmon-crested cockatoo
    11, 92
  vernal hanging parrot 86
  white-crowned parrot 86
peafowl (Indian) 78–79
peanut-headed lanternfly
  173
pigeons 84–85
  Nicobar pigeon 85
  Victoria crowned pigeon
    84
platypus 66
poison 66, 162–63
porcupine (bicolor-spined)
  63
possums 69
  common ringtail
    possum 69
  Herbert River ringtail
    possum 69
potto 28

predators 54,
  56, 62, 69,
  113, 116, 126
prey 22, 46, 48, 56, 60,
  80–81, 128

R

rainforest see jungle
reptiles 110–33
rhino (Sumatran) 56, 58
river turtles see turtles
rodents 62–65
rufous woodpecker 93

S

scales 18, 112, 150
scent 14, 25, 26, 28, 68,
  130
shrews 20–21
  common tree shrew
    20
  large tree shrew 21
  pen-tailed tree shrew
    21
  Philippine tree shrew
    20
siamang 37
sight 21, 31, 57, 80, 140
sloths 9, 16–17
  maned three-toed
    sloth 17
  pale-throated
    three-toed sloth 17
  pygmy sloth 16
snakes 113, 126–33
  bushmaster 133
  carpet python 127
  common boa constrictor
    128
  Cook's tree boa 129
  Ecuadorian coral snake
    130

emerald tree boa 8, 9,
    127
  green anaconda 126
  hognosed pit viper 133
  king cobra 132
  Malayan pit viper 133
  mangrove snake 131
  milk snake 130
  rhino viper 133
  white-lipped tree viper
    133
South American coati 45
spiders 160–61, 162–63
  Brazilian wandering
    spider 163
  funnel-web spider
  golden orb weaver
    161, 163
  huntsman spider 163
  and silk 162
  Thailand black tarantula
    160
spiny devil walking stick
    160–61, 165
sunbittern 83
superb fruit dove 85
superb lyrebird 103

T

tadpoles 136–37, 143,
  145
talons 81
tapirs 56–57
  Brazilian tapir 56
  Malayan tapir 57
teeth 49, 62, 128, 155
termite nest 18, 40, 43,
  44, 123
territory marking 14, 25,
  26, 28, 37, 47, 68

tiger (Bengal) 8, 9, 46
toads see frogs
toco toucan 96
  bill 96
tools 39, 40
tree frogs see frogs
tree shrews see shrews
tree snakes see snakes
trogons 94–95
  green-backed trogon 95
  narina trogon 94
  red-headed trogon 94
  resplendent quetzal 94
turtles 112–15
  alligator snapping turtle
    114
  Central American river
    turtles 115, 126
  common snapping turtle
    113, 114
  twist-necked turtle 115

U

understory 160

V

vertebrate 14
venomous bites 124,
  131–33
vipers see snakes

W

warm-blooded 14, 74
wattle 76
western tarsier 29

Z

zebra duiker 60
zoos 46, 85